The Cube of Space
Container of Creation

by Kevin Townley

Archive Press
Box 11218
Boulder, Colorado 80301

and

Editions Le Chaos
6100 Wilderton #12
Montreal Quebec
H3S 2L1

First published in 1993 by
Archive Press, Inc. and Editions Le Chaos

Archive Press
Box 11218
Boulder, Colorado 80301

Editions Le Chaos
6100 Wilderton, #12
Montreal Quebec
H3S 2L1 Canada

First Printing, 1993
© Kevin Townley, 1993

Library of Congress Cataloging-in-Publication Data
Townley, Kevin T.
The Cube of Space: Container of Creation/by Kevin Townley, 1st ed.
Bibliography: p.249

ISBN 0-9635211-9-5 hard cover

Cover illustrations by Michael Schussler
Figure illustrations by Chris High
Typesetting and cover design by Arts & Letters, Boulder, Colorado

I have brought thee before me for instruction
And whether thou receivest it willingly or unwillingly
Know that because thou hast this day heard or read
these words,
Thor art henceforth consciously united to me.

To-day thou mayest reject me.
To-day thou mayest receive these words with scorn.
Yet it shall be that my Voice
Shall go with thee henceforth forever

—*The Book of Tokens*

This book is dedicated to the joy of my life,
my two sons Kevin and Sean
and
My Holy Guardian Angel

As a treader of the Path for nearly 55 years, I have found the information in this book is very sound and clearly from an Internal source. I can think of no esoteric aspect that has not been explored in this very extensive work by Kevin Townley. This is a world-class book.

—*Joseph Norlan*
Editor of the Inner Journey

In the study of the Qabalah there is no more important a glyph than the Cube of Space, except for perhaps the Tree of Life.

—*Dr. Paul Foster Case*

This is without a doubt the most original and useful recent contribution to occult and Tarot studies. It is a brilliant synthesis of ideas which demonstrate for the first time the extent to which the Cube of Space is a coherent repository of interlocking symbolic ideas. It is a work which every student of Western Qabalah and of Tarot should be read.

—*Robert Wang*
Author of Qabalistic Tarot

Acknowledgments

Special thanks to my dear friend Rachel M. Walton, for her monumental, and continued support throughout this effort.

To my brothers Bill Van Doren, Scott Wilbur, John Townley, and Kenneth Miller, for their encouragement, and sometimes irritating attention to detail.

To my sisters Jane Craig, Karen Di Giacamo, Sandy Riely, Audrie Salmon, Barbara Grogan, and Elizabeth Ordell. To Connie Woodland and Marianne Gregory for those late night gematria extravaganzas.

Special thanks to Arlan Lazere for taking in strays.

To the Metaphysical bookstore and Bob Williamson who could always find the hard to find book.

To all my brothers and sisters of Denver Pronaos #501, Pat Adamson, Barbara Chavis, Irene Cumine, Doris Deering, Claudia Kuhns, Nicole Moody, Cherie Page, Bob Qualls, Vicky Schuessler, Kimberly Cass, Beverly Corbett, Ruth Cumine, Brian Jackson, Roger Lindenmuth, Traci Owens, Michael Schuessler, Karen Straight, Bob Williamson, Philip Wingfield, Mark Witkin, Lee Witkin and Don Zimmerman.

To all the custodians of the Builders of the Adytum who keep the flame burning, with special thanks to Len Jones, Joseph Nolan, Aheda Iannazzo, Fedda Rizzo, Brockton Hill, Kathleen Kemper, Margaret Ghazi, Rosenell Hetherington Roberta Iannazzo, Diane Rhodes, Marion Hills, Roger Cabanel, and in loving memory of Dr. Paul Foster Case, Dr. Anne Davies, and Gary Usher.

Many thanks to Chris High for his taking over the art work of this book, and burning the midnight oil, for Karen High for her work on the back cover, to Michael Schlusser for his loving gift of the front cover of this book, to Aziza Scarpelli, my dear editor, and to Don Zimmerman for getting me over the last proof-reading hump.

Heartful thanks to the folks at Arts & Letters, for the typesetting and for the layout of the cover of this book. Special thanks to Jay Nelson, Jan Bauman Kingsbury and Jim Applegate.

TABLE OF CONTENTS

INTRODUCTION

I was first introduced to the Cube of Space in a study group sponsored by the Builders of the Adytum (B.O.T.A.), in Boulder, Colorado. Its faces, lines and Tarot keys caught my attention like nothing else I have ever encountered. After studying with the B.O.T.A. for several years, I decided to go as deep as possible into the detail of the Cube of Space.

After some research, I found much to my disappointment, that there was nothing written on the Cube that would shed more light on the basic material already written by Dr. Paul Foster Case.

I contacted the B.O.T.A. office in L.A. and they informed me that there was no more material available on the Cube. As far as I know, the only detailed information concerning the Cube is written by Dr. Case. There is mention of the Cube of Space in Robert Wang's *Qabalistic Tarot* where a couple of paragraphs present it as an alternative system to the Tree of Life. In some of the different translations of the Sepher Yetzirah, there is a presentation of the Cube of Space, both by Carlo Suares, and Aryeh Kaplan.

Since there was no more written material to satisfy my desire, I decided to see if there would be any revelations through the power of concentration. As I began this endeavor I was amazed at what was revealed concerning the Cube of Space. Little by little the information began to build. It became apparent that there was enough material available to put into book form.

As this work evolved from a journal into a book I began to realize that the information gathered was not arranged for the beginner.

I remember reading *The Golden Dawn* by Israel Regardie and feeling frustrated by the 96 pages of introduction informing the reader of the list of books that must be read before attempting to take on the work of that particular text. It became obvious that the material in *The Golden Dawn* was not intended for beginners, such is the case with this book.

Anyone who has completed the first year and a half of study with the B.O.T.A. will be well-suited to understand this work.

The language of this text uses Qabalistic terms from the Tree of Life. It will be difficult to penetrate this work unless there is a basic working vocabulary in the Qabalah.

For the beginner wishing to investigate this work, I would recommend *The Mystical Qabalah,* by Dion Fortune, *A Practical Guide to Qabalistic Symbolism,* by Gareth Knight, and *The Qabalistic Tarot,* by

Robert Wang. There is also the courses of study offered by the
B.O.T.A. which deals with the language in depth. Although these
works overlap, they offer the different perspectives of the authors,
and they will give a basic understanding of the Qabalistic language
to the attentive reader.

The greatest recommendation I could make concerning instruction is the course material of the B.O.T.A., which takes the student from the beginning to a wealth of knowledge in just over a year
of study.

It seemed fruitless to write an introductory text on the Tree of
Life when so many fine texts are already available. Those looking for
an introduction into the Qabalah will find it in the sources mentioned above.

Some of the work in this book will stand firm against criti-
cism and the fires of trial and error; other parts may be replaced
with more durable insights. This work is certainly intended to open
up a rather large Qabalistic can of worms, which will inspire others
to look deeper into this topic, and hence bring forth the gems that
await those who enter into this domain.

Since there is little in the way of research material, I can say
that this work is a testimony to the powers of concentration which,
when rightly used, will reveal many exciting details about whatever
we choose to place our attention upon. This power of concentration
is the alchemical Mercury which brings all things into dissolution
and as a result opens up the inner nature of the object at hand. The
power of concentration is spoken of in the following quotation, in
the meditation on the letter Heh.

>Fix thy mind on the object set before thee by any letter,
>And hold thy thought to meditate thereon.
>Then shall the inner nature of that object
>Be made known to thee,
>And by this means shalt thou draw nigh
>To some aspect of my being.[1]

It must be said that this book is not intended to be a great
treatise of dogma, but a record of what is considered to be revelations received through the personal journey of the author, as conscious attention was placed on the structure of the Cube of Space. It
is believed that there is nothing else written on this topic which

deals with the Cube of Space in such detail, as is presented in this work. The reader will find a great deal of elaboration on the Cube where none previously existed in written form.

Work of this nature is always the result of the exhaustless efforts and dedication of those who have gone before us. As students of these mysteries, we have the trials and errors of our elder brothers and sisters, who left us with clues and signposts along the way to assist us with damage control. It is often tempting to take credit for realizations that have come, largely due to the foundations, clues, and leads brought forth by others; it is also important to mention the most sublime of all gifts, the State of Grace, without which we would still be hanging out in trees or holes in the ground, responding fearfully to the Directive Intelligence within whom we live, move, and have our being.

It is my sincere desire to share realizations, conclusions, or theories and, at the same time, acknowledge those wonderful beings who laid strong foundations which allow works such as these to come forth.

I used various approaches in order to open my mind to the influx of information that awaits any aspirant who prepares to receive it. Such approaches were meditation, working with models, living in models. I attempted to exhaust any intellectual conception I might have concerning the Cube of Space and, by virtue of their inseparable relationship, the Tree of Life.

Perhaps one of the most interesting experiences in the writing of this book took place in my bedroom. I was trying to understand the relationship between the diagonals of the Cube of Space, the sphere of Malkuth, and the invisible sphere of Daath. Having exhausted every intellectual recourse I had, I went to bed feeling greatly frustrated. At three o'clock in the morning I was awakened with a burst of inspiration concerning my question. As I got up I realized I was sleeping in a room that was nine feet wide, nine feet long and nine feet high. For the past two years I had been sleeping in a cubic room. When I stood up in the room, my physical heart was in the center of the cube, just as Tiphareth is at the center of the Tree of Life.

Although occult studies constitute a vast ocean of knowledge, there have been many streams that have generated this tremendous body of knowledge called by many names: the Qabalah, Hermeticism, Gnosis, or the Western Mysteries seem to feel most comfortable to me, yet other names could do as well.

It has been over ten years since I joined the B.O.T.A. and be-gan studying the works of Dr. Paul Foster Case. I was continually amazed at the humility and depth that this man brought forth in his exhaustless writings. He represents the greatest human influence to inspire the bringing forth of this work. With the groundwork and clues that Dr. Case left, this effort was launched into its present form. It is not my intention to place the B.O.T.A., Dr. Case, or his suc-cessor, Dr. Ann Davies, on the infallible chair of St. Peter, but to sim-ply say thank you and acknowledge their gifts to us.

It must be stated that this work has grown from the seed from which it was planted; namely, it is a product of the study with-in the B.O.T.A. as well as other texts which seemed to complement this work. It seems fitting to say that this work is a footnote to the writings of Dr. Case. The final straw that seemed to trigger, what I feel to be the congelation of this material was in *The Qabalistic Tarot,* by Robert Wang. It therefore seems appropriate to offer my sincere thanks to him as well.

Although this work is based on the studies of the B.O.T.A., it must also be said that it is independent in the sense that it relates to a personal experience and interpretation, which may not necessarily be in total agreement with the teachings of the B.O.T.A..

It is with humility and love that this work is shared both in-tellectually and heartfully. It is also the sincere desire of the author to perhaps add just one more trickle into this vast ocean called the Western Mysteries.

Here, dear reader, is, like the Tree of Life, a map of conscious-ness of The Cube of Space, for those on the path of return.

SUB UMBRA ALARUM TU ARUM
YOD HEH VAV HEH

Kevin Townley 1993

Permission granted for the use of its materials by the B.O.T.A. does not in any way endorse the interpretation of the author. Readers interested in pursuing the teachings of the B.O.T.A. may write to: Builders of the Adytum, Ltd., 5105 Figueroa Street, Los Angeles, CA 90042.

LIST OF FIGURES

Chapter Three

Chapter Four

Chapter Five

CHAPTER ONE

THE CUBE OF TRUTH

efore discussing the form of the Cube and its complexities, it is helpful to gain some understanding of the Cube's symbolic nature. We can do this by venturing over to a salt shaker and taking a close look at the grains of salt,[1] which are tiny cubes, then considering how we've come to regard salt. We know that salt can be used to clean and purify wounds, and that it is a good preservative for such foods as meat, fish, and vegetables. We also know that salt adds flavor to food and to the experience of eating. Some of our old sayings regarding salt shed light on the symbolic nature of the Cube. For example, we say that "he is the salt of the earth," when we encounter someone who expresses a genuine loving nature. The individual appears to be working in service for the good of the many. In contrast, when someone is known for spinning tall yarns or giving information based on insufficient data, we say, "When this guys speaks, you better take what he says with a grain of salt." The listener quickly understands that the story may well lack wholeness.

"Old Salt" is a term used to describe a sailor, someone who spends a great amount of time on the briny sea — a universal symbol for the collective unconscious. When we say that the salt of the earth has lost its flavor, we are saying that someone tends towards selfishness, does not work for the good of the whole, rather serves the personal self. In the same vein, Jesus said, "If salt should lose its flavor, it has no worth and should be cast to the ground and trampled under foot."

Now, let's take these sayings about salt and apply them to the Cube. The Cube is one of many well-known symbols for wholeness and truth, yet we must look at all sides of a cube in order to have a clear understanding of the truth we are seeking. As you know, one can only see half of a cube at any given time; the rest must be sought by maneuvering it about. We can say that someone "is working from only half a cube" when they don't have the whole story. To add "a grain of salt" to an argument is to add an entire cube of salt and, possibly, a solid, vital idea to it.

The Cube as truth (as in the principle of salt) is a purifying agent. It represents the reconciliation of opposites. In alchemy, salt is used to purify its opposite principle, sulphur. After the salt is purified by fire, it is added to the sulphur. The salt will absorb the impurities of the sulphur which can be eliminated from the salt by fire once again. The result of this exercise is the unification of these two principles in one homogenized form. It is in this operation that the balancing of opposites and the purification of the principles takes place. This is seen through the hermetic principle of polarity. It states,

> "Everything is dual; everything has poles; everything has its opposite; like and unlike are the same; opposites are identical in nature, but different in degree; extremes meet; all truths are but half-truths; all paradoxes may be reconciled.[2]

Cirlot's *Dictionary of Symbols* describes the Cube, "Among solid forms, it is the equivalent of the square. Hence, it stands for earth, or the material world of the four elements." Denis, the Carthusian, an English monk, pointed out that cubic objects represent stability because they are not capable of rotation as are spheres.[3]

If we refer to *Genesis* 1:2, we read, "Now the earth was formless and void;" this is certainly not the earth we have come to know. This statement adds a new dimension to our understanding of what the Cube of Space is about. The Cube is the limiting agent that defined a certain space and allowed the formless and void to become the formed, defined Earth. It is also the agent that fixes the life force of the Divine Mind within a particular center of expression. This allows a specific manifestation of the infinite potential of the One in a specific finite act. Thus, the Cube is the divine fixing agent that allowed the heavens and the earth to be separated, and remain in that state until the Divine Mind would bring them back into the formless and void state. Likewise, salt cubes preserve food until it is ready to be consumed.

The idea of preserving or defining takes us to the basic boundaries of the Cube. The Cube is defined by its limits: six faces, twelve boundary lines, and eight corners. It is a stable "platonic" solid that offers fixation and limits for divine expression.

Here are some key points to consider:

- The Cube represents truth and wholeness.
- It is necessary to have access to the whole Cube to understand the principle of polarity.
- The manifested universe, or the Cube, is based on love because it works for the good of the whole.
- The Cube preserves and defines a specific idea, an act of intention from the infinite storehouse of possibility.
- Without the cubic defining influence, an idea remains pure potential and is absorbed back into the unmanifest.

MASONIC SYMBOLISM OF THE CUBE

Without discussing Free Masonry at length, it is helpful to look at some of the masonic symbols concerning the cube. When an initiate enters into the "**Craft**," he is considered to be an "Ashlar," a rough stone that is removed from the quarry. The aspirant must be properly prepared for placement in the "Temple Made Without Hands." This rough stone becomes the perfected cube that will be used as a cornerstone. The masonic system of study and initiation is designed to bring the Ashlar to perfection. Thus, the Cube is also the symbol for perfected humanity.

If we look at the back of our one dollar bill, we will see the Great Seal of the United States. On the Great Pyramid, the top stone or capstone is missing. The placement of the capstone can only occur through Divine Grace, represented by the all-seeing Eye of God. This is another symbol for the perfected Ashlar, after the Master Mason has chipped away that which is not needed. This is the Sanctum Sanctorum, the Holy of Holies. The Ashlar connects the cube with the inmost portion of the Temple of Solomon which was twenty cubits cubed.

THE NEW JERUSALEM

In *Revelation* 21:15-16, the "Messianic Jerusalem" is described as a perfect cube:

> "The angel that was speaking to me, was carry-
> ing a gold measuring rod to measure the city
> and its gates and wall. The plan of the city is
> perfectly square, its length the same as its

breadth. He measured the city with his rod and
it was twelve thousand furlongs in length and in
breadth, and equal in height."

The same symbolism carries throughout the mysteries concerning the perfection of humanity. When Jesus said, "The Father and I are one," he placed the entire mystical process at our feet. The Father (AB) and the Son, Jesus, (BN) spells the word "stone" in Hebrew (ABN). The union of the Father and the Son creates the perfected Ashlar, the cornerstone for the "Great Temple Built Without Hands." This is the same stone which Jesus referred to as being "rejected by the builders as being of no worth."

This connection with humanity and the stone brings us back to the first chapter of *Genesis*. When the Elohim (God)[4] created man in their image and likeness, they did not create the perfected product any more than when we plant a seed we plant the completed flower. The Ashlar is in the image and likeness of the perfected "**Ehben**" stone, but it is not the finished product. The rough stone needs the work of a skilled craftsman in order to ready the stone for placement in the Temple, the **New Jerusalem.**

Returning to the concept of the Cube as a binding force that holds fixed an act of divine intention, it is necessary to turn to another of the seven hermetic principles, the principle of Mentalism. This principle states, "The All Is Mind, the Universe is Mental."[5] This principle tells us that everything that exists is of a mental nature before it proceeds into physical form. We have all been through periods of brainstorming when a multitude of ideas come and go through our minds. None of these ideas will have any concrete reality on the physical plane until we choose to focus our attention on one specific image. What we are actually doing is creating a "**space set apart**" from all other images that have no specific form. This space is the **Cube of Space.** We must then follow our image up with action. This creative process can be described as, "thought, word, and deed." First, we must extract one idea from the many ideas that flow through our minds. Then, there must be an act of intention where we speak the creative word. Finally, there must be action that will charge the intention which brings it into the manifested world. When we refer to *Genesis* 1:26, we can see this entire process unfold,

"And the Elohim said, "Let us make man in our
image, in the likeness of ourselves, and let them
be masters of the fish of the sea, the birds of

heaven, the cattle, all the wild beasts and all the reptiles that crawl upon the earth. 'God created man in the image of himself, in the image of God he created them, male and female he created them.'"

In this creative act, we see an intention to create something specific: man. In order for creation to take place, the object of focus must become specific. So how clear was the image of man in the mind of the Elohim? It was the image of themselves. Once clarifying the image, they spoke the creative words **"Let There Be."** Then there was the creative act, "He *made* man, male and female, He made them."

In order to bring an idea into manifestation, it is necessary to "Fixate the Volatile," as the alchemist would say, or use a preservative such as salt (the cube), the stable platonic solid.

The Sepher Yetzirah,[6] describes yet another creative act of the Divine Mind. In this particular story of creation, the symbolism of the Tree of Life and the Cube are used. This is a different story of creation than that in the Book of Genesis. It is a description of the boundaries of the universe that were created by the Divine Mind through the vehicle of expression of the Divine Mind. The name of this center of expression is Jah (IHV). This process is the fixing, limiting quality which sets a space apart from the infinite potential for the sake of manifestation. The Cube of Space and the Tree of Life are produced when the Divine Mind desires to manifest its creative ideas in the world of name form.

The divine intention begins at a point of focus in the form of a particular idea. This idea takes on the same energy form as that of the spiral nebula or the centripetal rotation of a galaxy. This whirling vortical motion is the beginning of the creative process. This process is referred to in the Qabalah as "the beginning of the whirlings."[7]

There are two basic directional flows of energy: one moving outward from the center, and the other moving inward towards the center. The movement outward is the divine impulse to create, to express; the flow back towards the center is the urge within the created centers of expression for unity with the Creator. These movements are known as centrifugal and centripetal motion. In relationship to the path of return, these forces are referred to as involutionary and evolutionary. These forces are a result of the creative intention coming forth from the mind of the "All."

As a center of expression is created, it takes on a sense of separation from the One. As the center emanates further and further away from conscious connection to its source, the sense of separation becomes greater. This is known as the path of involution. At some point during this involutionary descent, a center of expression develops an ability to become "Awake." As this awakened state increases, the sense of separateness and self-determination decreases. At some point in the involutionary phase of the creative cycle, the consciousness of a particular center of expression changes direction. This awakened state and change of direction, is the beginning of the evolutionary path or **Path of Return.**

At this point, the center of expression shifts focus from one of personal identification to one of understanding and integration with the greater reality. This is the identification of being an agent and directed instrument of the **Absolute.** The shift of focus does not mean that the individual center has a working knowledge from experience of this reality, rather it undergoes a change from selfish seeking for the sake of receiving, to seeking experience of the **True Self** for the sake of **Serving,** and thus giving.[8] At some point in this selfless seeking for the True Self, a center of expression will have firsthand experience and verification of the **Greater Reality.** When this experience occurs, there is a fixation of the volatile and most sublime consciousness of the Absolute. The particular center of expression becomes a direct conscious agent for the **Will** of the **One.**

This is the completion of the **Great Work.** It is the final preparation for the Ashlar to be placed within the Holy Temple, **Made without Hands.**

From an act of intention, solidified in a creative image, centers of expression develop in experience in order to become ever greater instruments for the **Absolute.** Figure 1 shows this cycle of Involution and Evolution.[9]

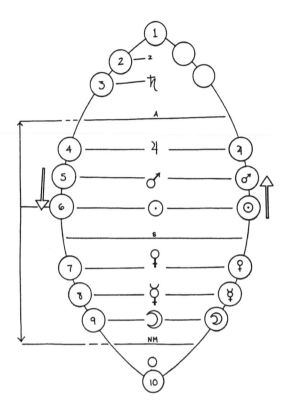

Figure 1
Involution/Evolution

The left side of the diagram shows the descent of conscious-ness, from unity into apparent separation. This is the phase of invo-lution where a center of expression becomes immersed in form and develops skills in becoming a specific expression of the Divine Mind.

The tenth sphere shows the line of demarcation where a cen-ter of expression shifts direction from separation or descent to unifi-cation and ascent.

At this point, we are concerned with the movement from the center outward. Now any force moving from a center outward, such as a series of ripples created when a stone is thrown into a pool of water, will decrease in power as it continually expands. Constant ex-pansion finally results in non-expression. When ripples come in con-tact with a barrier, the influence of the ripples can be felt. Anyone who has ever encountered the wake from a large ocean going vessel can attest to the severe impact on a small boat. In the creation of the universe, according to the *Sepher Yetzirah*, Jah created the necessary boundaries in order to establish an impact of the creative forces upon its centers of expression. It is the formation of these barriers that allows us to experience the creative mind of God through the twelve signs of the zodiac. These twelve signs are the twelve lines that define the boundaries of the cube.

The six faces are bounded by six of the seven sacred planets known to the ancients. The seventh planet, Saturn, rests at the center. All of these barriers or boundaries are set up so the Divine Mind can experience itself in a fixed form for as long as it chooses to. Now, the divine expression, Jah "sealed" the six directions by changing the order of the letters in his name or by using the six permutations of (IHV). Numerically described as 1x2x3=6. In six stages did Jah inscribe His name. First, the above, below, east, west, south, and north. All of this activity took place from a center. It is at the center where the intention is formed. The intention generates a whirling vortex, which expands outward, from the center, seeking limits and expression. This originating principle is associated with the sphere of Kether, The Crown of Primal Will. The center of the Cube and the sphere of Kether are one and the same.

The Divine Name, Jah, is associated with the second sphere of the Tree of Life. Chockmah, Wisdom, is said to be the sphere of the zodiac, and its influence is carved into the six faces, eight corners and twelve lines of the Cube by the six permutations of (IHV). It is here that we find a strong connection between the influence of Chockmah, the twelve signs of the zodiac, and the use of the cubic principle salt as a fixing agent. It is the principle of salt, an inherent quality of the sphere of Binah, where the divine potential of Chockmah is made manifest. Following are some relationships which show the connection of Chockmah to the Cube through the use of Gematria.

Chockmah is called the sphere of Mezla, the Holy Influence. Mezlah is the outpouring of the intelligence of the twelve signs of the zodiac. The value of Mezlah is 78. Notice that the number 78 reduces to 15, the number of the shortened version of Jah (IH) attributed to Chockmah.

(MZLA) - Mezla. To drip or flow down in drops; influence; whirling radiant energy.

(MLCh) - Melek. Salt; to subsist.

(ChLM) - Kohlem. To bind.

The color attributed to Chockmah is grey, the color of balance, and the color attributed to the Cubic Stone. Ehben, the word for stone has a value of 53. Besides meaning "The Father and the Son are One" (mentioned earlier), there are few words of the same value that enhance the idea that there is great power in the stone and that the stone is a binding force.

(H-GDVLH) - Ha Gedulah. The majesty, the magnificence.

(ChMH) - Khammaw. Sun, heat, to bind or join; to enclose.

(GN) - Gan. Garden, wall enclosure.

(BTChV BIHVI) - Biteku Ba-Jehovah. Trust in the Lord.

The stone is also the place where Jesus said he would build his church. The Latin word Ecclesia, meaning church, has the value of 53, as does Ehben, stone.

Chockmah is the first emanation from the Crown of Primal Will. Of itself, it has no specific expression until it comes in contact with its polar opposite, Binah, the Great Mother. As Chockmah is the sphere of the zodiac, Binah is the sphere of Saturn. It is through the qualities of the sphere of Saturn that manifestation is made possible.

To form a square, a fourth point is needed. There is a location on the Tree of Life for this point yet there is no visible sphere located here. More will be said of this point and the invisible Sphere of Daath later.

We can say that Kether is the Crown of Primal Will and all acts of Divine Intention spring from this first point.

Chockmah, the first emanation from Kether, and the second point, is the seat of the Life Force, the sphere of the zodiac where the Divine Intention is charged, directed, and projected into a space where it becomes limited by a specific idea or clear image.

Binah, the Great Mother, and seat of the Divine Soul is the third point. It is the form-giving sphere where the divine impulse is clothed in the necessary image.[10] These three spheres are the Supernal Triad found in the archetypal world, where the pure possibility of the Divine Mind is transformed into a creative image. These three points allow knowledge of where an impulse originates, what its possibilities are, and where it is going.

This knowledge gives rise to another quality of the Divine
Mind: its placement on the Tree of Life is not visible. It can be located geometrically, yet it is not considered to have a sphere of influence as do the other ten spheres. This invisible sphere will be
considered in more detail later on, as some interesting points are
brought forth about the sphere of Daath, Knowledge.

This fourth point on the Tree creates the formation of a
square in relation to Kether, Chockmah, and Binah. Since all of these
aspects rest in the archetypal world, they can be referred to as "that
which is above," as they form the top portion of the Cube of Space.
In relation to the Cube, it is the above face which is the first face or
direction sealed by Jah.

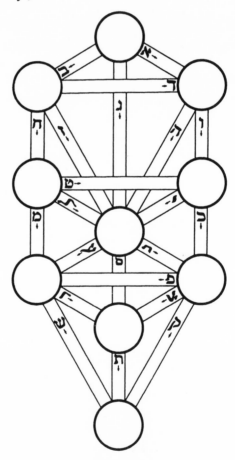

Figure 2
The Tree of Life

In the Catholic Church, the sacrament of confirmation is given to children as they enter their 12th or 13th year of age. It is said that the Holy Spirit descends upon all those confirmed and they would receive the seven gifts of the Holy Spirit. These gifts are: wisdom, understanding, council, knowledge, fortitude, piety and fear of the Lord. It is not necessary to go through the process of associating each of these gifts with the spheres of the Tree of Life, but it is useful to call attention to the first four gifts and their relation to the second, third, and invisible sphere of the Tree, Wisdom, Understanding, and Knowledge. Even though the sacrament of confirmation is cloaked in religious dogma, the cube of truth emerges when one looks closely.

The following diagram is a model of the Tree of Life with the Supernal Triad marked to show the formation of the upper face of the Cube. The invisible sphere of Daath is used to inscribe one of the corners.

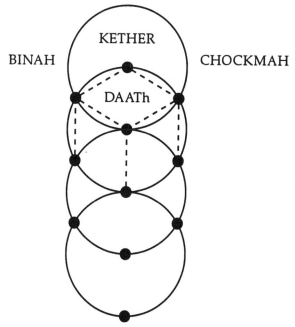

Figure 3
Formation of the Cube of Space on the Tree of Life

The particular example of the cube inscribed on the Tree is a microcosmic aspect of the universal Cube we are studying.

In *Sepher Yetzirah* 1:11, we read,

> "He selected three letters from among the simple ones and sealed them and formed them into a Great Name (IHV), and with this He sealed the universe...."

The symbol of the universe or Macrocosm is the "Mogen David," the Star of David, the hexagram. When the points of the hexagram are connected, we have a hexagon, and when the center point of the hexagram is connected with two of the points, i.e., Chockmah and Binah, we have the Cube.

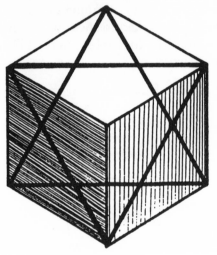

Figure 4
Formation of the Cube of Space through the Hexagram

The symbol of the Macrocosm is formed by six circles of equal diameter centered around a central seventh circle of the same diameter. This is referred to by Dr. Case as THE SECRET OF THE COSMOS AND NUMBERS.[11] It is within this symbol that the Universal Cube of Space is formed as well as the Great Pyramid of Cheops and the seven-sided vault of Christian Rosenkreutz. According to Case, "It is the key to all geometrical forms." If the six circles tangent to a central seventh were projected into three dimensions, it would be twelve spheres tangent to a central thirteenth. When we look at this particular idea, different religious doctrines can be understood. Jesus was the center of twelve apostles. There are twelve signs of the zodiac, and each individual person is a center receiving their influence. The earth, in this case, is the main sphere considered as being at the center of zodiacal influence. The following is a model of the six circles tangent to a central seventh creating the hexagram, the Tree of Life, and the Macrocosmic Cube of Space.

In this figure, you can see (as in Figure 4) the hexagram of two equilateral triangles. The central line which bisects the two equilateral triangles is the middle pillar of the Tree of Life. The Tree of Life is outlined by the tangent points on either side of the central row of circles. Each of the four circles represents the four worlds of the Qabalah: the archetypal, the creative, the world of action, and the world of form.

The outlined cube at the center, is the central Cube of the Macrocosm and is the square root of the larger Cube.[12] This smaller cube is the center of expression where the Divine Intention is extended to its designed limits, so that it may express itself in finite form. Notice that this central cube is inscribed within the central circle which is tangent to the six outer circles. This, of course, is a two dimensional explanation of a three dimensional idea. As we begin to understand some other aspects of the Cube, we will move into a three dimensional evaluation.

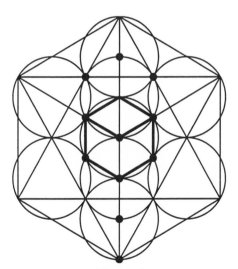

Figure 5
Six Circles tangent to a Central Seventh

As the detail of the Cube becomes more involved, it appears more foreboding. Most of my fellow aspirants have resisted studying the Cube because of the complexity of lines, letters, astrological symbols and geometrical forms. There is a simplicity about the Cube when first looking at the solid structure. To be truly involved in the process of studying the Cube, there is the usual work that one needs to face in taking on any new area of study. Approaching it in sections seems to work best. The great challenge is taking this form, and bringing a practical application to the quest of spiritual enlightenment. The Cube, like the Tree of Life, can give us a finite understanding about the infinite Mind of the One Life, and how it is that we are created in the image and likeness of that **One Being.**

At this point, we can return to the *Sepher Yetzirah* and begin to investigate and explain the sealing of the Universe in the form of the Cube.[13] This process begins with reference to Figure 5 and brings our attention to the central cube that rests at the center of the Macrocosm. It is here that the projector of the Universe begins with the Divine Act of Intention. In Verse 9 of Chapter 1, it speaks of the Spirit as being first.

> "First; the Spirit of the God of the living;
> Blessed and more than blessed be the Living
> God of ages. The Voice, the Spirit, and the Word,
> these are the Holy Spirit."

Now, the Holy Spirit is attributed to the third sphere on the Tree of Life. The Holy Spirit is also called the quintessence of the alchemists and akasha of the system of Yoga. "From akasha all things come and to akasha all things return." Pure Spirit or the quintessence is said to be the first matter of the alchemists, so all things derive their growth and increase from the Spirit/Quintessence. The Pure Spirit has its roots in the Unmanifest or the Ayin Soph Aur. It finds expression in the Creative Mind of the All. It is through the womb of the Great Mother, the Holy Spirit, that the Unmanifest takes on its various robes of beingness.

In Verse 10, we read,

> "Second: from the Spirit He produced Air, and
> formed in it twenty-two sounds - the letters,..."

It is here that the element of air is created. In *Genesis* 1:2 we read,

> "The Creative powers of the Life Breath were
> hovering over the waters."

(RVCh) is translated as Spirit and is also referred to as "The Life Breath". With the prefix of the letter Vav (V), it gives the intimation of the union of Spirit and the element of air. Air is emanated from Spirit before any other element. It is the first elemental force used to define the Cube. It was the Spirit of God that moved from the center, sealing the above and the below. In the Chaldean or Hebrew Aleph-Beth, Aleph is associated with the element of air, and it has no sound save the vowel points that are given to it. It is, therefore, attributed to the line inside the Cube that connects the above and the below to the center. This also brings into play the three modes of consciousness. Superconsciousness is connected with Aleph, self-consciousness is associated with the above face of the Cube and subconsciousness is attributed to that which is below.

Continuing with Verse 10 of the *Sepher Yetzirah*, it says,

> "Third; from the Air He formed the Waters, and
> from the formless and void made mire and clay,
> and designed surfaces upon them, and hewed
> recesses in them, and formed the strong material
> foundation."

Mem (M) is the second of the three Mother letters, Aleph being the first. It is these waters that are referred to in Genesis 1:7. Mem, Water, is the line inside the center of the Cube that extends from the center to the east and from the center to the west. The east being the direction where the sun rises and the west where the sun sets.

Fourth; from the Water He formed Fire and made for Himself a Throne of Glory with Auphanim, Seraphim and Kerubim, as his ministering angels; and with these three he completed his dwelling, as it is written, "Who maketh his angels spirits and his ministers a flaming fire."

The letter Sheen (Sh) is the third of the Mother letters and has its placement moving from the center to the north and the south. These three mediums or axes appear to cross each other at the center to form a three-armed cross. In fact, there is an instant projection originating at the center and terminating at the designated boundaries.

The cross formed by these three axes, can be seen in the cross of the Eastern Orthodox Church. Esotericaliy, it represents the sealing of the six directions from a seventh central point. The following diagram illustrates this.

In this Figure, we can see where the three Mother letters are located and connect the three lines that extend from the center to the six faces.

The three Mother letters (A, M, Sh) were the means used to seal the six directions. By virtue of the polarity of the directions of Mother letters, the seven double letters were formed. These double letters are associated with the seven sacred planets known to the ancients. They are the physical embodiment of the hermetic principles of polarity, for each of these letters has a dual expression.

Figure 6
The sealing of the Six Directions with the three Mother Letters

In the sealing of the six directions, the Divine Will chose three simple letters to form the name Jah (IHV).

In Verse 11, the *Sepher Yetzirah* continues:

> Fifth; He looked above, and sealed the Height
> with (IHV).

The height, or above, is a symbol of self-consciousness. It is given the letter Beth, whose double meaning is Life and Death. In our self-conscious state, we need to live the awakened life. Ignorance and lack of attention create the environment for stagnation and sickness which creates death. On the other hand, knowledge and keen observation allow a transparent expression for the "One Life," which in turn creates health and immortality.[14]

> Sixth; He looked below, and sealed the Depth
> with (IVH).

The letter Gimel and the planetary attribution of the Moon reside on the below face of the Cube. It represents the subconscious level of expression. Peace and Strife are the polarized expressions for this letter.

Seventh; He looked forward, and sealed the east
with (HIV).

This is the location of the letter Daleth and the planet Venus.
ts double meaning is Wisdom and Folly. It is associated with the sun-
·ise and the beginning of a particular cycle of creation. The letter
)aleth and the planet Venus are associated with creative imagination.

Eighth; He looked backward, and sealed the
west with (HVI).

The direction west is the place of completion of a particular
:ycle in the creative process in the mind of the All. The planet
·upiter and the letter Kaph are assigned here. Wealth and Poverty
·re the double meanings of this letter. This is the sense of reaping
·ne's "just desserts" according to the particular seeds that were
)lanted in the east. The east and west (D, K) emanate from the cen-
·er of the Cube through the agency of the Mother letter Mem, and
:ompletes the polarity of the rising and setting Sun, thus Light and
)arkness.

Ninth; He looked to the right, and sealed the
south with (VIH).

The south is the place of warmth and sunshine. The letter
Resh and the heavenly body of the Sun are associated with the south.
Fertility and Sterility are the polarized meanings of the letter Resh.

Tenth; He looked to the left, and sealed the north
with (VHI).

The planet Mars and the letter Peh reside in the north. Iron,
·he metal of Mars and the polarized expression of Grace and Sin are
·lso aspects of the northern face of the Cube. The northern face com-
·letes the sealing of the six directions. The north also balances the
·olarity of heat, associated with the south, through its opposite, cold.

The last verse of Chapter One makes a statement that con-
·ects the Cube to the Tree of Life.

Behold! From the Ten ineffable Sephiroth do pro-
ceed – the One Spirit of the Gods of the living,
Air, Water, Fire; and also Height, Depth, East,
West, South and North.

The Cube is, indeed, a product of the Tree of Life, and this
·will be dealt with in greater depth later on in this work.

Thus far, we have seen the extension of the elemental forces, outward from a central point to a particular boundary. These elemental forces arise from the three Mother letters Aleph, Mem, and Sheen. Their boundaries are created by the six faces of the Cube: above-below, east-west, south-north. The diagram below shows the extension of the three Mother letters, and their connection to the six faces of the Cube.

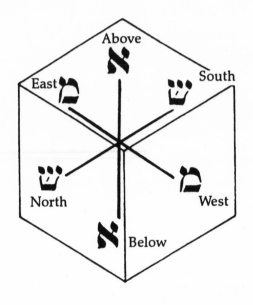

Figure 7
The Mother Letters sealing the six faces of the Cube of Space

From the whirling vortex of Kether and the fiery Life Force of Chockmah, the vessel of Saturn (Tav), in the sphere of Binah, sets up the conditions for the limits of the six directions. It is from this place that the Divine Being Jah, a pre-involutionary aspect of Jehovah, sealed the six directions from a central seventh point. It is the working of the Divine Father (potential) through the agency of the Divine Mother (limitation) that allows this to take place.

The seven spiritual planets represent seven limited ways in which the One Life records its intelligence in the world of form. The Holy Influence (MZLA) is the outpouring from Chockmah, which fills the planets and allows their specific expression by means of the twelve boundary lines of the Cube of Space. We also note that each ice of the Cube, with a planet at its center, is bound by four lines, a umber that is symbolic of the square and, thus, order. This states at the creative act is one of order as opposed to the chaos from which divine expression emerges.

You will notice that each face of the Cube has boundaries in common with other faces of the Cube. This creates a special relaionship between these faces, which will be discussed later.

In Chapter Five of the *Sepher Yetzirah*, the Twelve Simple Letters are placed on the Cube. Each letter representing a zodiacal sign. ach sign finds itself directly opposite the letter/sign which is opposite it in the zodiacal year. These are the holy influences that stream rom the stars and have their roots in the sphere of the zodiac, 'hockmah (Wisdom).

As each line binds two faces together, so each line is described by the two faces it contacts; for example, the first of the Simle Letters Heh (H) is located on the northeast line of the Cube. The northeast line holds the quality of the northern face assigned to Mars and to the eastern face assigned to Venus. The southeast line of he Cube, assigned to Vav (V), connects the planet Venus and the outhern face assigned to the Sun. The following diagrams show the Cube with its zodiacal attributions.

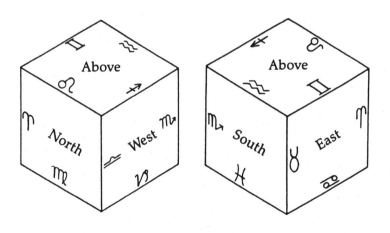

Figure 8
The placement of the Zodiacal signs on the Cube of Space

Before any manifestation takes place, there is total unity. This unity transcends gender and the idea of duality. This unifying consciousness is located in the sphere of Kether. Within this unity there exists the potential for polarity, yet in this particular state, it is latent and unmanifest. At the center of the Cube, we find the idea of unity. From this unity or point emanates the Divine Will to experience itself in a multiplicity of ways and forms, which result in seeming polarities. From this point, at the center of the Cube, come the three Mother Letters which extend to the six faces of the Cube. Each face has its opposite, which is grounded in the same Mother Letter as its opposite. Each face is further bounded by four edges, which are attributed to the zodiacal signs. From a central point to the formation of the boundaries of the Cube, the One Life, which is infinite, experiences itself in finite ways.

The following is a list of the names of the letters and their places on the Cube.

The Three Mother Letters

Aleph (Uranus) - Extends from the center to the above, from center to the below. (Element of Air)

Mem (Neptune) - Extends from the center to the east, from the center to the west. (Element of Water)

Sheen (Pluto) - Extends from the center to the south, from the center to the north.

The Seven Double Letters

Beth (Mercury) - Above face.

Gimel (Moon) - Below face.

Daleth (Venus) - eastern face.

Kaph (Jupiter) - western face.

Resh (Sun) - southern face.

Peh (Mars) - northern face.

Tav (Saturn) - Center or Holy of Holies.

The Twelve Simple Letters

Heh (Aries) - northeast corner.

Vav (Taurus) - southeast corner.

Zain (Gemini) - east above.

Cheth (Cancer) - east below.

Teth (Leo) - north above.

Yod (Virgo) - north below

Lamed (Libra) - northwest corner

Nun (Scorpio) - southwest corner

Samek (Sagittarius) - west above.

Ayin (Capricorn) - west below.

Tzaddi (Aquarius) - south above.

Qoph (Pisces) - south below.

The following diagrams show the six faces of the Cube with their planetary attributions in the center of each face, and the zodiacal signs around the twelve boundary lines.

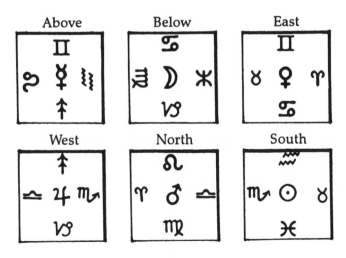

Figure 9
The Six Faces of the Cube of Space

THE GNOSTIC CROSS

The symbol of the Gnostic Cross is the Cube unfolded with its zodiacal attributions written on each line and planetary attributions in the center of each square. This is the Cross of the Gnostics who were later labeled as heretics by the Orthodox Church. This particular Cross is a symbol of what the Master Jesus meant when he said, "We must take up our cross daily." The Gnostic Cross is also a symbol of the integration of the twelve zodiacal forces and the seven sacred planets. The seventh planet is not present on this cross because it resides in the center of the Cube, the (Holy of Holies).

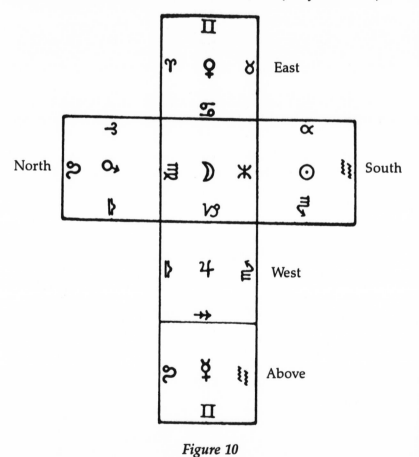

Figure 10
The Gnostic Cross

These last two diagrams show the Cube in its separate parts.

All that is necessary to put the Cube together is to line up the corresponding zodiacal signs.

When one studies the Cube one face at a time, it becomes simpler to understand and memorize its structure.

In the sealing of the six directions, it is interesting to note the process that unfolds in the Divine Being, Jah. This aspect of the Most High, seated in Chockmah, transforms from a boundless limitless being of potential, to one who creates limits for its expression. With the addition of the twelve lines, eight corners, and the six faces, we have the number twenty-six, 12+8+6=26. This number exceeds the value of the name Jah by five. Five is the value of the letter Heh. With the addition of the letter Heh to the name Jah, we have Jehovah, who was the Creator in Genesis. It is also important to remember that the letter Heh is assigned to the sphere of Binah, the sphere of the Divine Mother. Binah is also the sphere of Saturn, limitation and form.

The value of Jah is twenty-one and this is the value of the name Eh-Heh-Yeh-Heh. This name is associated with the first Sephiroth Kether, the Crown of Primal Will. Jah is the first emanation of the Primal Will and contains the latent unmanifest quality of Kether, but is seated in Chockmah. When this name binds itself with the boundaries of the Cube, it becomes transformed from formlessness to that which is defined. It is defined by the universal boundaries, namely the signs of the zodiac, the seven sacred planets, and the four elements.

It is at this point that the story of Genesis is able to unfold. Here the Projector of the Universe has set up the arena in which the world can be made manifest, and a space was created where highly developed centers of expression could grow from a creative idea to the manifest forms that we now experience as humanity. From the infinite possibility of the Ayin Soph Aur, to the binding quality of the creative image, to still more defined expression as in humanity, the Divine Mind creates vessels, centers of expression, where it expresses itself in myriad finite ways.

THE NATURE OF SOUND

"Through sound the world stands." This is one of the doctrines held by the eastern tradition of Yoga, and sound corresponds to our Spirit and Quintessence. The Holy Spirit is associated with the sphere of Saturn. The first movement of the Spirit associated with the sphere of Saturn was to create the twenty-two letters of the Chaldean alphabet. The sound quality of these letters is the binding force of the Cube. Because of the nature of the letters, the Cube has a holding power, a fixing power. Each letter contains its own vibratory force, and finds expression throughout the universe. Within our star system, these letters find expression through the twelve signs of the zodiac, and the planets within our solar system.

It is the quality of the letters that forms us, guides us, and influences us. It is the force by which we aspire towards conscious unity with the Divine Mind. These letters, as mentioned earlier, are given a particular attribution of a sign or a planet. In simple astrology, the observation of the planets and their movements around the Earth and their positions in the zodiacal signs, gives us insight into the nature of the individual.

The same is true for the Cube. The sphere of the zodiac, Chockmah, contains all of the influence of the twelve signs and brings that influence to bear on the boundaries of the Cube. Mezla (MZLA), the Holy Influence, descends from Chockmah. If we were to break the word Mezla down into its parts we would find (MZL) Mazawl, and (LA) Lo. Mazawl is the word for planet, or wanderer. Since the time of the fall to self-consciousness, from the Garden of Eden, we have been wanderers, seeking the source from whence we came. LO, means No-thing, from which the involution of form took place. The reversal of the word LO, OL, or AL is the most simple form of the word for God, the God of Mercy and Compassion. Together these two words speak of the holy influence that shows us that the No-Thing gives its bountiful influence through the sphere of Chockmah to the wanderers who seek entrance into the Holy Temple, or to the center of the Cube. The exterior of the Cube is the vestibule (AVLM) of the temple, whose value is 77, the same as that of Mazawl. It is through movement around the perimeter of the Cube that the wanderers, or planets, gain access to the Holy Influence. With the integration of these influences we become ready to enter the temple and, hence, the center of the Cube. This is analogous to the twelve labors of Hercules, that were required before balance could be restored to the world. Upon completing these labors Hercules became immortal.

From the moment Adam and Eve were expelled from the Garden of Eden, they became wanderers and needed to actively embody Divine Consciousness. At the time of the fall, they were unable to express these integrated qualities in their newly awakened state.

THE CURRENTS OF THE CUBE OF SPACE

One has choices at certain times as to which of the exterior lines of the cube they will travel. It is much like traveling on a river. There are currents to deal with, eddies to rest in, and inlets to explore. In certain places, you must simply follow the current and face the experience. On the exterior of the Cube, there are various directions in which the energy flows. The following diagram shows this movement.

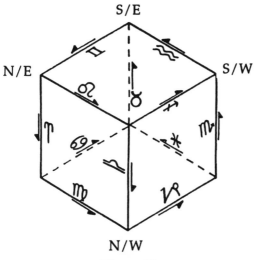

Figure 11
The Currents of the Cube of Space

On the above face of the Cube, the energy flow moves in a counterclockwise direction. The eastern face flows in a clockwise direction. The northern, southern and western faces take on a different movement. On the northern face the above and below line flow from east to west. The northeast and northwest line descend from above to the below. In the southern face, the above and below lines flow from west to east. The southwest and southeast lines ascend from the below to the above. The western face has the above and below lines flowing from the north to the south. Since the northwest, and southwest lines have already been explained, we can see that the west has an ascending and descending line. Descending in the north and ascending in the south.

It is on the bottom face of the Cube that challenges come to light. The flow of energy moves in a clockwise direction from the north below line to the west and then to the south. It is the east below line which breaks the flow of energy, for it moves counterclockwise, from north to south.

What does all of this mean? It is the ride on the river of life, and the path of return. You can at times chose which river you want to travel, but you must follow its currents and go where it leads. In some cases, you need to travel a couple of different rivers in order to get to the one you are seeking. Each river has its own challenges. Some are easier to travel than others. Some bring us face to face with our fears of separation and death.

In dealing with the Cube as an evolutionary process, we must travel all of its rivers in order to get to the source.

We have become self-conscious beings since our biting into the apple in the Garden of Eden. The above face represents the self-conscious state. It is here that we begin our journey to the center. The four lines that bind the above face of the Cube take us around and around until we choose to accelerate our evolutionary process. Once we do this, we are never the same.

When we hear the calling, and choose to make a difference in our lives, we descend into the subconscious world of memory, and return into consciousness with the gems that await the courageous traveler. When we choose to jump into the river, we begin the most exciting journey there is, the path of return to the Most High.

There are two places where we can gain access to our subconscious levels. They are located on the northeast and northwest corners on the Cube. These are the zodiacal signs of Aries and Libra.

Imagine it is the twenty-second of March, the time when the Sun enters the sign of Aries and the Vernal Equinox. At this time, the Earth's energies are in balance and a new zodiacal year begins. If we were to take this point of time and refer to the Cube, we would find ourselves at the northeast above corner. Here is a place to begin our descent, our wanderings around the boundaries of the Cube. This is a crucial point on the Cube, for the energy flow can either take us down into the lower face or allow us to continue to circumnavigate the above face. If we refer to the diagrams that show the Cubes energy flow, we can begin to map out our journey.

As we descend the northeast line, we arrive at a point of choice. We can travel from east to west via the path of Yod, Key 9,

The Hermit, and the astrological sign of Virgo; the other choice is to travel from north to south, through the current of Cheth, Key 7 the Chariot, and the sign of Cancer. If we choose the line of the north below, Virgo, we must travel through the north face to the western face, and the western face to the southern face. At the southwest corner, we have the opportunity to surface through the sign of Scorpio, for here there is access to the above face. If we continue, we must traverse the southern face traveling from west to east. Here we will be forced to surface due to the merging currents of Cancer and Pisces, which drive all travelers to the surface through the path of Taurus.

The different planetary forces represent our different modes of consciousness. Those familiar with the Tree of Life will already know the attributions given the four cardinal directions, for they are the same as the spheres on the Tree that bear the same planetary name. The north is assigned to Mars, the sphere of Geburah. The east is Venus, assigned to the sphere of Netzach. The west is Jupiter and assigned to the sphere of Chesed. There is a slight difference in the relationship between the Sun assigned to the southern face of the Cube and Hod, which is the sphere on the Tree. For those who wish to challenge this point, the author asks their patience until it is dealt with later on in this text. For now, Hod will gain the association of the southern face. The basic introduction to the Cube is almost complete.

One other major point needs to be addressed: Our journey around the faces of the Cube eventually lead us to the center. This is the goal. Within the interior of the Cube lie four lines that connect each of the four below corners of the Cube to the four above corners diametrically opposed. These diagonal lines correlate to four of the five Final Letters of the Chaldean Aleph-Beth. These four letters take on a special form and significance when they are placed at the end of a word. These are Final Kaph, Nun, Peh, and Tzaddi. It is through these Final Letters, and the path which they represent, that one is able to enter the center of the Cube. When one reaches the center, they have access to any face on the Cube, as did the Divine Father Jah when He sealed the six directions from the center.[15]

The following diagrams show the diagonals moving from the below through the center to the opposite corner.

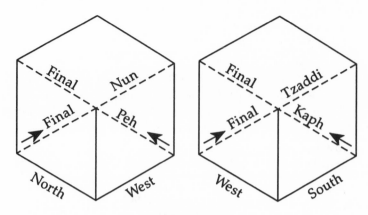

Figure 12
The four Finals

The first figure shows the extension of Final Nun moving from the northeast below corner to the southwest above corner. It also shows Final Peh moving from the southwest below corner to the northeast above corner. The second diagram shows Final Tzaddi moving from the northwest below corner to the southeast above corner. Final Kaph ascends from the southeast below corner to the northwest above corner. Each of these diagonals pass through the center of the Cube. The center of the Cube represents the Holy of Holies. From the center, one can see the entire cube and move to any face at will. This is the place of perfection, completion and the "Administrative Intelligence." It is also the place where the fifth Final Letter, Mem, rests.

Together with the letter Tav, they spell the word Toom (TM), meaning completeness, perfection. Toom has a value of 440 when (M) is valued at 40. Also the value of 440 is (ChZChzITh)-wheelings, circling, and (ShKL KLLI) the Collective Intelligence, the intelligence associated with the Sun and the letter Resh. The diagonals are only accessible from the lower faces of the Cube.

To arrive at Final Nun, one only has to descend the northeast line of Aries and take the diagonal to the southwest above face.

To arrive at Final Peh, you would descend the northeast corner, traverse the north below line, then to the west below line until you reach the southwest below corner.

To arrive at Final Kaph, one descends through the northeast corner and once traverses the east below face until arriving at the southeast corner.

To arrive at Final Tzaddi one descends the northeast corner and travels west to the northwest below corner.

Final Mem is at the center. The first of the Final letters is Kaph and it is the first to be traveled. Before one may travel to the center, the western face must be experienced. It is on the west below line that Key 15 lies. Key 15 represents the shadow, The Devil, the dweller on the threshold. The same is true of the other letters. They, too, must be integrated. To arrive at the final letters, one must integrate the regular form of the letter.

This completes the basic introduction to the Cube of Space.

FOOTNOTES

[1] Throughout this text, **SALT** will be used as a principle and is not
  necessarily (NaCl) table salt. Salt as a principle is a fixing
  agent, as well as a means of purification of the other two principles, **Mercury** and **Sulphur.** Salt also represents the physical
  body. In this present description, table salt is being considered
  primarily because of its obvious availability and the general
  understanding of its use.

[2] *The Kybalion* by Three Initiates

[3] *A Dictionary of Symbols* by J.E. Cirlot. Philosophical Library.

[4] Elohim: "The masculine plural of the feminine singular. Derived
  from (AM), the arabic, meaning mother, and the creative principle. Elohim is the Divine Name attributed to Binah, the Third
  Sepherah. It is more representative of the multiple ways God
  expresses, rather than multiple deities. In this case, Elohim is
  used in relationship to the creative principle of the Mother.
  There are other references to Elohim as being lesser gods, angels, or even spiritually evolved members of humanity." Gesenius: P.428-433; 517.

[5] The Kybalion, by Three Initiates

[6] *The Sepher Yetzirah* is perhaps the most celebrated of Qabalistic texts.
  Its origin is not definitively known, yet it is the the source of
  both the geometrical forms of the Tree of Life and the Cube of
  Space. *The Sepher Yetzirah* is the main source for this present text
  on *The Cube of Space.*

[7] TOL-10-1 by Dr. Paul Foster Case

[8] *The Power of Aleph-Beth.* Philip S. Berg.

[9] *Fundamentals of Esoteric Knowledge,* Lesson 2, Page 13, LPN-USA.
  Translated from the French lessons of Les Philosophers de Nature, Malesherbes France, by Brigitte Donvez, Editions le Chaos.

[10] The pure potential of Chockmah needs a vessel in which to express itself. Binah and its power of limitation clothes this potential of Chockmah within the form of an image, a specific
  idea.

[11] *The Tarot,* A Key To the Wisdom of the Ages. Paul Foster Case. Macoy Publishing Co. Richmond, Virginia. 1947

* The Cube of Space is formed by the limiting power of the sphere of Binah, and the planet Saturn. A cube of 9 units which is manifested on the earth has a square root of 3, the number of the sphere of Binah.

* In this context, the term sealing is used to denote the limits imposed on an act of intention, and the creative image, from the infinite storehouse of potential.

* *GW* by Dr. Paul Foster Case.

* *TF-44:5* by Dr. Paul Foster Case.

* *TF-44:5* by Dr. Paul Foster Case.

CHAPTER TWO

THE PRINCIPLE OF CORRESPONDENCE

"t is true, certain, and without falsehood, that whatever is below is like that which is above; and that which is above is like that which is below: to accomplish the one wonderful work. As all things are derived from the One Only Thing, by the will and by the word of the One Only One who created it in His Mind, so all things owe their existence to this Unity by the order of Nature, and can be improved by Adaptation to that Mind.

"Its Father is the Sun; its Mother is the Moon; the Wind carries it in its womb; and its nurse is the Earth. This Thing is the Father of all perfect things in the world. Its power is most perfect when it has again been changed into Earth. Separate the Earth from the Fire, the subtle from the gross, but carefully and with great judgment and skill.

"It ascends from earth to heaven, and descends again, new born, to the earth, taking unto itself thereby the power of the Above and the Below, thus the splendor of the whole world will be thine, and all darkness shall flee from thee.

"This is the strongest of all powers, the Force of all forces, for it overcometh all subtle things and can penetrate all that is solid. For thus was the world created, and rare combinations, and wonders of many kinds are wrought.

"Hence I am called HERMES TRISMEGISTUS, having mastered the three parts of the wisdom

of the whole world. What I have to say about the
masterpiece of the alchemical art, the Solar
Work, is now ended."[1]

This is the **TABULA SMARAGDINA HERMETIS,** The Emerald Tablet of Hermes. It is a statement about the relationship of the **One** force of the Divine Mind and how it manifests itself through its centers of expressions. This tablet refers to the hermetic principle of correspondence. This law is stated thus,

"That which is above is as that which is below,
and that which is below is as that which is above."

We can take this principle and apply it to the flow of energy that descends from Kether to Malkuth and back to Kether. "It ascends from earth to heaven and descends again to earth reborn." We can see this principle of correspondence come into play as we study the Tree of Life, and the descent of the Cube of Space through the Tree. We can also see the descent of the Tree of Life through the Cube of Space.

The Emerald Tablet speaks of a power that is integrated into all things if it be turned into earth. This power is the pre-existent quality which transends our comprehension. In Qabalistic terms, it is the Ayin Soph Aur. These are the three veils of negative existence which exist above or outside the spheres of intelligence of the Tree of Life. This is the Chaos from which all forms emerge. It is in fact the "All." This infinite boundless being desires to express itself in finite ways. This process of expression begins in what is called "the three veils of Negative Existence." It is called negative since it transcends space and time, it has no specific quality, and it lies beyond our ability of comprehension.

The veil above Kether is **Ayin, The No Thing or Nothing.** This veil is referred to in the First Chapter of Genesis, when we read, **"In the beginning God created the Heavens and the earth."** Now the word **Create,** means to manifest something out of **Nothing,** or to make something from a creative image.

The next veil is the Ayin Soph, and means **No Limit.** The name Ayin Soph Aur, **THE BOUNDLESS LIMITLESS LIGHT** is the third veil. For a greater understanding of these concepts, refer to *The Mystical Qabalah,* by Dion Fortune, *A Practical Guide to Qabalistic Symbolism,* by Gareth Knight, and *The Qabalistic Tarot,* by Robert Wang.

The very best we can do in our efforts to know the mind of
the All is to understand some part of the All, as its intentions con-
dense through the four worlds of the Qabalah.

None hath seen Me face to face,
For I am the forerunner of all.

Thus, O Israel, am I ever before thee
On the way of Life,
And to all mankind it is said,
Even as to Moses:
"Thou shalt see my back parts,
But my face shall not be seen."[2]

Since we are a product of the creative principle in the mind of
the All, we can gain some knowledge of the All by studying its creations, and the laws that govern creation on the physical plane,
which lie below the veils of negative existence.

Kether is the first sphere on the Tree of Life. Kether is the
fruit of the condensation of a creative impulse of the mind of the
All, just as Malkuth is the fruit of the beginning of the whirlings established in Kether. We can say that Malkuth is to Kether as Kether
is to the Ayin Soph Aur.

In the *Sepher Yetzirah*, we read ten and not nine, ten and not
eleven, are the ineffable Sephiroth. Kether is one and Malkuth is ten,
$10=1+0=1$. Kether is in Malkuth and Malkuth is in Kether, but in a
different manner. (The relationship between 1 and 10, or Kether and
Malkuth, will be referred to several times as we proceed with the
work on the Cube and the Tree.)

If we ascend from earth to heaven, Malkuth to Kether, we can
gain an understanding about the relationship between the Ayin
Soph Aur and Kether. The principle of correspondence shines
through when we contemplate the letters of the negative veils (AIN
SVPh AVR).

The relationship between the negative veils and the Ten
Sephiroth are quite interesting when the letters of the Ayin Soph
Aur are considered as Sephiroth on the plane above the world of
Atziluth. Imagine that. These letters can be considered as a more
subtle condensation of the intelligence of the All. If we were to take
the letters of the negative veils and place them on an identical diagram of the Tree of Life, the principle of correspondence would be
brought into play. Figure 1 shows this relationship.[3]

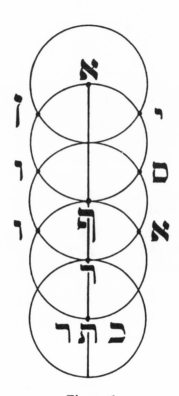

Figure 1
The condensation of Chaos into the sphere of Kether

Notice that there are nine letters in Ayin Soph Aur (AIN SVPh AUR). These letters fill the first cycle of numbers, 1-9, and terminate in the tenth sphere of Kether. Kether continues the condensation of the chaos into the archetypal world. Referring to Figure 1, we can see that Kether does not begin the process of creation but is a stage in the process, just as Malkuth is. Kether is a result of the same laws that generate the spheres below Kether. "**As above, so below.**"

This relationship between Kether and the Ayin Soph Aur, can be made more clear when one addresses the construction circles of the Tree of Life.

If we take a clean sheet of paper, we have a working model of the Ayin Soph Aur. There is nothing on the paper and there is no limit to what can be expressed upon that sheet.

By taking a pencil and placing a point anywhere on the paper, you will have created a center of expression.[4]

From this point, a series of circles are drawn. Each of the numbered circles represents one of the four worlds of the Qabalah. The above circle which holds no number is the circle associated with the Ayin Soph Aur. The Sephiroth are then placed in the proper position.

Each of the construction circles has a unique relationship with the circle above and below it, for they pass through the center of each other. This passing through the center creates a geometrical form called a **vesica**. This vesica is the container by which the intelligence of one world is transformed into the world below it.

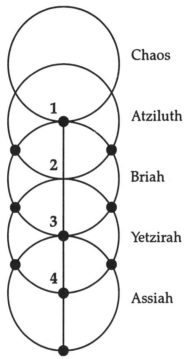

Figure 2[5]
The construction of the Tree of Life, and the Four Worlds

There are usually four construction circles used when drawing the Tree of Life. In Figure 2, there are five. If we bring our attention to the number 1 and the sphere of Kether, we will see that it is the only sphere located on the vesica of the Negative Veils. It resides at the lowest tangent point on that vesica. Since it is located on the vesica of the Negative Veils, it must partake of their qualities. It must act as a transition point from the **Nothing,** to the **Something.** As we have seen in Figure 1, Kether is, in fact, the Malkuth of the Negative Veils.

This relationship of transition continues as we descend our conventional Tree of Life.

The second vesica is located in the world of Atziluth, the archetypal world. Within this vesica, we have the spheres of Kether, Chockmah, and Binah, along with the invisible sphere of Daath. These spheres receive the influence of the Ayin Soph Aur through the agency of Kether, and begin the process of solidification. Now the archetypal world is far from solid, according to our experience, yet it is more specific than **Nothing**. As the intelligence of the Negative Veils fills the spheres of the world of Atziluth, the undifferentiated potential becomes differentiated potential. It is still, however, potential.

Continuing our descent of the Tree, we come to the vesica of the Briatic world, the world of creative ideas. The upper tangent point on this vesica is the invisible sphere of Daath. The other three spheres are Chesed, Geburah, and Tiphareth. Daath is the agency which delivers the archetypal intelligence to the creative world. It is here that some point of focus of the differentiated potential is placed within a vessel of creative imagery. As this specific image draws upon the unlimited potential, a **Space** is set apart for the manifestation of form. Before the form can come into being, there must be a creative act in the world of Yetzirah.

Tiphareth is the sphere which delivers the creative intelligence to the lower spheres of Netzach, Hod, and Yesod. Tiphareth is the uppermost point on the Yetziratic world, the world of action. Tiphareth holds a special relationship to all other spheres on the middle pillar, which act as transition points from one world to another.

Finally, Yesod brings the world of action into the world of form. It is Yesod that sets the stage for physical manifestation in the sphere of Malkuth and begins the next cycle of descent.

Malkuth is a good place to stop. We could theoretically take a trip to hell if we continued our descent. It is this book's intention to work on **The Path of Return**, not descent.

NUMBERS, NUMBERS EVERYWHERE

My secret wisdom is hid in number,
And in the sign of the Tally
Is concealed the building of the whole Creation.
Number veileth the power of the Elohim,
For number is that thick darkness whereof it is
written,

"And Moses drew near unto the thick darkness
Where God was"; and again,
"Tetragrammaton said that he would dwell
In the thick darkness"[6]

Consider the **Point**, and the three geometrical forms, the triangle, the hexagram, and the enneagram. The point and these three forms are representative of the first sphere Kether, the third sphere Binah, the sixth sphere Tiphareth, and the ninth sphere of Yesod. These forms and, hence, their numbers bring us to a very important consideration concerning creation.

Jah created the universe using numbers, letters and sounds.[7] The words Ayin Soph Aur contain 9 letters, Ayin Soph contains 6, and Ayin contains 3 letters. When taking these three numbers, 9, 6, and 3, we find that they hold a special function in the creation of the universe. In fact, there are only four real numbers: 1, 3, 6, and 9. This, of course, sounds absurd at first; yet if we look beyond the surface of appearance, we find this to be true. All other numbers are different expressions of 1, 3, 6, and 9.

Indeed, everything is **One** because all things come from **One**, as the Emerald Tablet states. The All is One. One is the undifferentiated and infinite possibility, and its reflection gives rise to the expression of the Father, the Number Two.

The All is three because the One Life always expresses itself through the Trinity or the Supernal Triad. The union of One and its reflection, 2, takes us from the negative veils of undifferentiated potential to the world of differentiated potential. This gives rise to the idea of the Trinity, 1+2=3, and the vehicle of the Mother, the vital ingredient for manifestation. The union of these forces are 1+2+3=6, and this brings us to the third of the four numbers of creation, 6.

The All is six, as it expresses itself through the agencies of the Divine Mother and the Divine Father, where the six directions of the Cube of Space are sealed, bringing forth a new generation, the **Son/Sun**. Furthermore, it is through the process of separation, or division, that manifestation comes into being. If we were to take the number 3, the number of the Divine Mother and sphere of Saturn, and divide it by .5, we find the number 6, the sphere of the Divine Son/Sun.

The All is nine, for there are nine letters in the third veil of Negative Existence and nine is also the number which completes the cycle of numbers. Nine is also the product of the Magic Square of the Divine Mother, 3x3=9. After nine, we return again to the number one and the cycle begins all over again and continues on infinitely.

At this point, we have become familiar with the basic cycle of numbers from one to nine. In esoteric sciences, the numbers from one to nine are used for mystical studies. There are other areas in the study of number that speak to the creative process of the Ayin Soph Aur and the numbers 1, 3, 6, and 9.

Kether is the tenth aspect in relationship to the Ayin Soph Aur, which is the line of demarcation between negative existence and positive existence. This begins the cycle of numbers at a new level of expression.

Now let's consider the statement that there are only four real numbers, 1, 3, 6 and 9, and that all other numbers are expressions of one of these four numbers. As there are four worlds in the Qabalah, there are the four levels in which numbers manifest. They are called: apparent, reduced, extended, and root numbers.

Apparent numbers are quite simply the numbers we use on a day-to-day basis, and are symbolic of the world of Assiah. This is exemplified in the Tarot by the suit of Pentacles, and Key Fifteen, The Devil, sign of cardinal earth. The hand of the Devil is in a position which says, "What you see is all the reality there is."[8] We need to look beyond the surface of appearance to gain the whole truth of a matter, just as we must maneuver a cube in order to see all its sides.

Any number being dealt with has an apparent value. This explanation is not an attempt to disregard apparent numbers but alert us to the fact that much more lies beneath the surface.

Reduced numbers are symbolic of the world Yetzirah, and are mostly used in the science of numerology. This is the reduction of any multi-digit number to a single digit. This reduces otherwise complex digits to a common ground in order to gain an understanding of the basic quality of the otherwise infinite. For example, the number 358, reduces to 3+5+8=16, 1+6=7. Through reduction, the number 358 can be expressed as the number 7. This process is called **Theosophical Reduction.**

Extended numbers, symbolic of the Briatic world, allow us to examine the greater relationships between numbers. Extending numbers is called **Theosophical Extension.** Through theosophical extension, we can see the total influence contained within a number and its underlying relationship between different numbers and words of the same value. This process is used most extensively in

he science of gematria, where relationships of letter and number are
explored. An example of this can be seen in the number 4 - adding
number fours total value, we find that the number 4 extended has
he value of 10, 1+2+3+4=10, and 10= 1+0=1. This tells us that the
number 4 and 10 have a profound relationship with each other and
they each express a unique quality of the number 1, just as each cen-
er of expression manifests the essence of the One.

There are a couple of formulae that allow the student to find
he extended value of any size number, as well as reversing the
process to discover what a particular number is an extension of. To
find the extension of a given number, use the following formula.

$$\frac{n \times (n + 1)}{2} = \text{extension}$$

We will use the example of 31, which is the value of EL,
Lamed + Aleph, the divine name given to the fourth sphere on the
Tree of Life, Chesed. The name means God.

$$n = 31, n + 1 = 32$$
$$\frac{31 \times 32}{2}$$
$$\frac{992}{2} = 496$$

496 is the extension of 31.
496 = the value of Malkuth.

This tells us that the extension of 31, is the extension of the
creative powers of God, manifesting in the sphere of the earth,
Malkuth, 496.

The following formula shows how to reverse the process, that
is, find what a particular number is an extension of.

$$\frac{-1 + \sqrt{1 + 8n}}{2}$$

Let n = 496
$$\frac{-1 + \sqrt{1 + (8 \times 496)}}{2}$$

$$\frac{-1 + \sqrt{3969}}{2}$$

$$\frac{-1 + 63}{2} = 31$$

Root numbers associated with the Atziluthic world, tell us that there is an underlying unity in all things, and that the One has three basic modes of expression. The following numerical chart reveals the four types of numbers.

Apparent:	1	2	3	4	5	6	7	8	9	10	11	12	13
Reduced:	1	2	3	4	5	6	7	8	9	1	2	3	4
Extended:	1	3	6	10	15	21	28	36	45	55	66	78	91
Root:	1	3	6	1	6	3	1	9	9	1	3	6	1

Now each number in the last horizontal row is the result of an extension, and then reduction of a number, which reveals the numbers of 1, 3, 6, or 9. In the first two rows, the numbers remain identical from one through nine. Once they go beyond single digits, the apparent numbers take on their own form while their reduced value brings them back within the one through nine number cycle.

The third row takes these numbers and shows their quantitative value, and expresses them in a multi-digit form when it applies. The final value in the last row takes the quantitative value and reduces it to a single digit which reveals the series 1-3-6-1-6-3-1-9-9. This series goes on infinitely. Now if we take this one step further and break the series into its trinitarian expression (1-3-6), (1-6-3), (1-9-9), then add the sum of each group, we find that the trinity always expresses the one, 1+3+6=10, 1+0=1. Each of the three groups reduces to one, and the **One** expresses itself through 3.

$$(1+3+6)=10, (1+6+3)=10, (1+9+9)=10$$
$$1 \quad + \quad 1 \quad + \quad 1 = 3$$

"All things are from One by the mediation of One, and all things have their birth from this one thing by adaptation." The One Life is the root of all existence and is continually expressed through the Trinity.

THE LAW OF TETRAGRAMMATON

There is a sequence of numbers that have a root value of 1. This can be seen in the number chart on the previous page. If we refer to the line of root values, we will see that the numbers 1, 4, 7, 10, and 13 all share the common value of 1, and therefore share a special relationship. This particular number series, 1, 4, 7, 10, 13... creates an environment for a very specific cycle of manifestation. This cycle of manifestation is called the **Law of Tetragrammaton**.[10] Tetragrammaton was the name used in more ancient times to refer to Jehovah. It was against Mosaic Law to utter the Ineffable Name of Jehovah aloud.

Ayin, the first veil of the Absolute takes its influence and impregnates Kether with an act of intention. "As above, so below." The intelligence of the first veil, Ayin, takes form in the supernal Triad. The supernal Triad takes the numbers 1, 2, 3, (Kether, Chockmah, and Binah). This forms the Trinity symbolized by a triangle with a fourth point in the center, as seen in Figure 3.

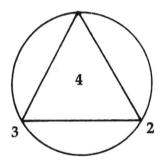

Figure 3
The Fire Triangle of Tetragrammaton

The numbers 1, 2, and 3 are placed on the three vertices of the triangle, with the number 4, being placed at the center. The number 4 becomes the seed for the next stage in the process of creation. The sum total of the value of four is 1+2+3+4=10, 1+0=1. We see that the number 4 is the first in the numerical series that returns to the number one. This first triangle is the fire triangle. It has been given the attributions of positive, masculine qualities.

Continuing with the series, we take the seed generated from the first triangle which is 4, and bring it to bear on the exterior of the second triangle. The initial number 4 still expresses the initial quality of the first triangle 1, but on a different level. The numbers 4, 5, and 6, reside on the points of the second triangle and the number 7 rests in the center. Remember that the extension of 7 is $1+2+3+4+5=6+7+28$, $28=2+8=10$, and $1+0=1$.

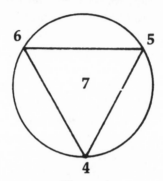

Figure 4
The Water Triangle of Tetragrammaton

    This triangle is a reflection of the first, and is expressed as the polar opposite of the first triangle. Hence, we have a triangle associated with the element of water, the feminine principle and negative pole.

    This particular sequence continues with the number 7 moving from the center of the second triangle to the apex of the third triangle, with the numbers 8 and 9 placed on the other two vertices. The number 10 is then placed at the center and becomes the seed which begins the next series.

    This triangle is associated with the element of air and has a neutral quality in relationship to the first two triangles.

    The air triangle is also associated with the divine offspring, the Son and/or Daughter.

    This series continues infinitely. We will limit our examination of this series to the numbers 10, 11, 12, residing on the points of the fourth triangle and the number 13 holding the center. This creates the triangle attributed to the element of earth, and represents a polarized expression to the air triangle.

    When we take the positive fire triangle, and the negative water triangle and bring their forces together, we have the expression of the Macrocosm. The same is true for the third and fourth triangles, as they are joined together.[11]

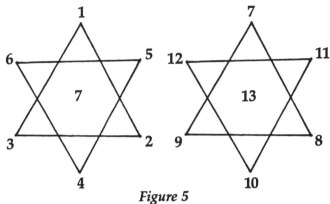

Figure 5
The union of elemental forces forming the Hexagram

The number 13, could be used to initiate the new cycle. Since each number at the apex of a triangle and the number at the center has a root value of one, we can surmise that the One is the initiating force, and that it is at the same time always centered in every act of manifestation. The triangles pointing upward are the volatile elements, fire-air, and ascend from earth to heaven. The down-pointing triangles are the heavier elements, water-earth, that descend from heaven to earth.[12]

The numbers on the triangles could be substituted by the letters in the Divine Name Jehovah.

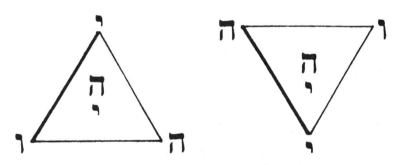

Figure 6
The Letters on the Fire and Water Triangles

The first letter of Jehovah, Yod, is the active projective principle and sits at the top of the triangle of the first series, as did the number 1. The letter Heh, which is attributed to the feminine principle and the sphere of Binah, sits at the lower right angle. The union of the Father and Mother or the Yod and Heh has a value of 15: Yod=10, Heh=5, 10+5=15. Fifteen (15), when theosophically reduced, 15 has the value of 6, 1+5=6. This is the value of the letter Vav. Vav is also attributed to Tiphareth, which is associated with the Son/Sun. Yod-Heh-Vav (YHV) is the spelling of the Divine Name Jah, who projected the limits of the Cube of Space in Chapter 1:11 of the *Sepher Yetzirah*. Upon completing the sealing of the six directions from a central seventh point, Jah added a fourth letter to His Name. Now IHV, has a value of 21. The Cube of Space has 12 lines, 6 faces, and 8 corners: 12+6+8=26. Twenty-six (26) is the value of IHVH, and 26-21= 5, the value of Heh, which is the fourth letter of the name of IHVH. The addition of the fourth letter, Heh, transforms IHV from a being of potential to a being who limits expression within finite vessels.

The name IHVH is now completed. The second Heh is placed at the center of the triangle.

The second Heh, brings a new quality to the Divine Name, Jah. This letter becomes the seed or new initiating principle for the next series, and transforms itself into the letter Yod at the apex of the next triangle, as did the numbers 4, 7, 10, 13, . . ., which are always expressing the number One. The letter Heh when spelled in full has a value of 10, Heh+ Heh, 5+5=10, and 10 is the value of the letter Yod.

If we were to take the number values of the two triangles, we would come up with the number 52. Yod-Heh-Vav-Heh, which has a value of 26 and 2x26=52. This is the value of (BN) Ben, son; (AMA) Aima, mother; and (BKL) Bekal, from all, in all, among all. It is also the value of Jehovah when each letter is spelled out (IVD-HH-VV-HH). If we were to connect the points of the hexagram as we did in Chapter One, we would, of course, have the Cube of Space.

These triangles, as formed by the name Jehovah, also have their involutionary and evolutionary process on the Tree of Life. As we descend from the above to the below, the density of spirit becomes greater and produces the fruit of the Tree, known as Malkuth. The following diagram shows the descent of the hexagram through the spheres of the Tree.

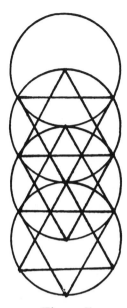

Figure 7
The Descent of the Hexagram

Before closing this section on numbers, there are a few relationships that need to be drawn. First, the number three associated with
the sphere of Binah has a root value of six. This brings together the
idea that the Mother, Aima, whose value is 52 is one with the Son, Ben,
whose value is also 52. Not only are the Father and Son one, as exemplified in the word (AB), but the Mother and the Son are one as well.

Second, the number 6 , the sphere of Tiphareth has a root value of 3. Notice the reflective quality of the sphere of Binah, the
Mother, in the sphere of Tiphareth, the Son, and from the sphere of
Tiphareth back to the sphere of the Mother, 1+2+3=6. Tiphareth, the
sixth sphere, 6, is 1+2+3+4+5+6=21, and 2+1=3. The combined influence of the Mother, 3, and the Son, 6, is 3+6=9, the value of the
sphere of Yesod. The numbers 1, 6, and 9 include the spheres on the
middle pillar of the Tree. 1= Kether, 6= Tiphareth, and 9= Yesod, the
sphere of the Moon. The number 3 is the form-giver, represented by
the Great Mother and the planet Saturn. Without the sphere of form
and limitation, nothing can be made manifest.

The numbers 3, 6, and 9 are also related. The number 1 is, of
course, the central idea. The number 3 is the working of the Trinity.
Both numbers 6 and 9 are the doubling and squaring of the number

3: 3+3=6, 3x3=9. It is the reflective quality of the sphere of Saturn that gives rise to the sphere of Tiphareth, and it is the squaring of the sphere of Saturn that brings forth the sphere of Yesod and, hence, the world into manifestation. It is specifically the squaring quality of the sphere of Saturn that we will delve into next.

Each sphere on the Tree has a Magic Square that reveals great secrets about the nature of that particular sphere. The exceptions to this are the first sphere Kether, and the second sphere Chockmah. Kether's value is one, 1x1=1. It is total unity, for it is the first condensation of the Absolute and, therefore, cannot be compared with anything other than itself because it is everything in itself. As Kether observes itself and sees its reflection, it gives rise to the number 2. To square the number 2, we end up with the number 4. In order for a square to qualify as a Magic Square, the sum of the horizontal, vertical, and diagonal lines must all be equal. If we were to take the square of 2 and create a square with four equal cells, we would find that the sphere of Chockmah would not meet the requirements. The following diagram shows why this is so.

Figure 8
The Square of Chockmah

The diagonal lines reveal 5 and 5. This works. When we add the bottom horizontal line we get 7. The above horizontal line reveals 3. The vertical lines show 6 and 4. It is clear that Chockmah can not meet the requirement for the Magic Square because like Kether, it has no definite quality. It is not until we arrive at the sphere of Binah, whose number is 3, and is the extension of the powers of Kether and Chockmah, 1+2=3, that we have the form necessary to create the first Magic Square. It is through the sphere of Binah that our Sacred Cube is manifested. The Magic Square of Saturn gives us 9 numbers, 3x3=9. Not only does Binah give us form, but it includes the entire cycle of numbers from 1 through 9.

1	2	3
4	5	6
7	8	9

Figure 9
The Square of Saturn

It takes 9 months for the gestation of a human fetus. It takes 9 years and 9 months for Saturn to complete 1/3 of its journey around the heavens. On the Tree of Life, the 9th sphere is the sphere of the Moon and is called "The Foundation." The Magic Square of Saturn is the foundation of the manifested universe and, hence, the Cube. Let us now take a close look at the Magic Square of Saturn.

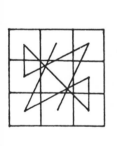

4	9	2
3	5	7
8	1	6

1	2	3
4	5	6
7	8	9

ר	ט	ב
ג	ה	ז
ח	א	ו

Figure 10
The Magic Square of Saturn

In the small figure to the right, we see the square of Saturn. It is not magic because the sum of its numbers are not equal in every direction. On the top horizontal line, for example, the sum is 6. On the bottom line, the sum is 24. But with careful rearrangement of the numbers, we can create the Magic Square. Notice that in the other diagrams the sum is always equal to 15. The large central diagram however, shows the actual Magic Square using Arabic numerals. The smaller square to the left shows the sygil of Saturn. The sygil of a Magic Square shows a pattern where each number moves through an evolutionary process in a particular Magic Square. As a new, higher number moves into the square, the lowest number moves out. For example the first Magic Square has the numerical sequence of 1 through 9. To continue the process, we can drop the number 1 and add the number 10 thus, having a sequence of 2 through 10. There are still 9 numbers. When a new number is added and an old number leaves, the total value of the Magic Square of Saturn is increased by 9, which is the square of Saturn, or 3 x 3 = 9

The lower diagram of Figure 10 shows the Magic Square with the Chaldean letters in the magical order.

The sum of those numbers is fifteen in any direction, and this is the value of Jah (IH), the Divine Name attributed to Chockmah. The total value of the Magic Square is forty-five. This is the value of Adam (ADM), generic humanity. This is also the value for spirit of Saturn (ZZAL), as well as the intelligence of Saturn (AGIAL). It is indeed the sphere of Saturn where all ideas congeal into the universal substance and become manifest in the word made flesh.

If we were to access the Latin gematria, we would find other interesting correspondences. Forty-five (45) is the value of Deus (God), Demon (devil), and Homo (man).

If the sphere of Saturn is the form-giver, then the Cube, which is a vessel, must contain Saturn's innate quality. Alchemically, Binah, the sphere of Saturn, is the principle of salt, and salt is the symbol for the Cube. The following diagram is the Magic Square as it appears on the Cube.[13]

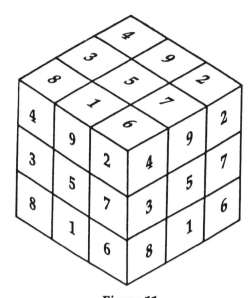

Figure 11
The Magic Square of Saturn on the Cube of Space

At first, the Magic Square of Saturn may appear to be a picture of Rubic's Cube, but it is actually the flowing of the numerical
sequence in involution and evolution. As the energy of the supernal
triad becomes more dense, the Magic Square of Saturn forms into
the physical plane, Malkuth, the fruit of the Tree of Life. Looking
closely at the Thirty-Two Paths of Wisdom, we see that the influence
of the sphere of Saturn is finally terminated in Key 21, The World,
whose attribution is the planet Saturn.

Just as Kether is produced by the nine letters of the Ayin
Koph Aur, Malkuth is produced by the nine spheres of the Tree of
Life. In Chapter I, Verse 12, of the *Sepher Yetzirah*, it states, "Behold!
From the Ten ineffable Sephiroth do proceed- the One Spirit of the
Gods of the living, Air, Water, Fire; and also Height, Depth, East,
West, South, and North."

The Cube of Space is defined by the emanations of the Mother letters as they move from the center and create the six directions.
The Cube comes from the Ten ineffable Sephiroth, as stated in Chapter 1:12. The following shows the Magic Square of Saturn with the
Chaldean letters in each of the cells.

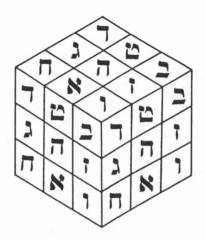

Figure 12
The Letters on the Magic Cube of Saturn

If we study the energy flow of the sygils as they move upon each face, we can see that the masculine faces, the above, north and south, are part of one line originating in the north, the place of darkness and the unknown. It moves from the north to the above, and ends in the south. There is no direct connection, at least by letter or number sequence, to the feminine faces, the below, east, and west. The energy flow follows the same pattern as the masculine, but moves in a different direction, namely from east to below, and is completed in the west. As seen in Figure 13.

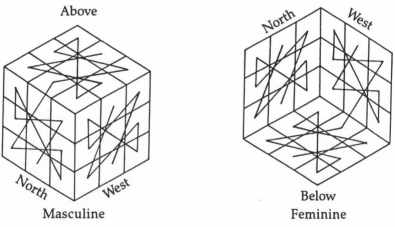

Masculine   Feminine

Figure 13
The movement of the Sygil of Saturn on the Cube of Space

There is yet another pattern that is quite remarkable. It
peaks to the combined efforts of the Law of Tetragrammaton, the
ix circles tangent to a central seventh, as well as using the building
lock numbers 1, 3, 6, and 9. It is a profound example of the Emerald
ablet of Hermes, and addresses the law of limits expressed in the
phere of Saturn. Once the limits are set, the enviroment is created
vhere the intelligences of the other Sephiroth may be expressed. As
he forms are defined, they maintain a common center and, at the
ame time, create new boundaries for ever greater expression of infi-
ite potential.

The form begins as the Tree of Life. There is first the point, a
ne drawn through the point, and then a circle inscribed around the
ne with the point in the center.

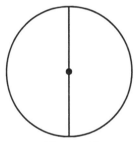

Figure 14

At the top of the circle, another circle is drawn, as with the
onstruction circles of the Tree of Life. Where the circles intersect, a
esica is formed. At each point of the vesica, another circle is in-
cribed. This process is continued until there is a six-pointed flower
ormed within the center circle, and six circles emanating from the
enter, one from each petal of the flower.

Figure 15

In the first series of circles, we have six circles flowing through the center of the center circle, a total of seven circles. The seven circles complete the first full cycle of the Law of Tetragramma ton, which can be seen in Figure 15.

The point of the compass is placed where the six circles inter sect each other, creating another series of vesicae. Another group of circles are then drawn. This series inscribes an additional 6 circles, bringing the total number of circles to 13.

Figure 16

After repeating this cycle once again, there would be another 6 circles drawn, giving us a total of 19 circles. The final 6 circles in this series creates the "Key to the Cosmos and Numbers," or the 6 circles tangent to a central 7th.

Within the nesting of this form, are 12 other circles which cre ate a web of six-petaled flowers, and the seeds for the next extension of the form. The nineteen circles brings us to an even greater expres sion of the Law of Tetragrammaton.[14]

Figure 17

The 19 circles form the Cube of Space in which the Magic Square of Saturn can be seen. By connecting the tangent points of the construction circles, the nine cells of the Magic Square are defined. The Magic Square of Saturn is the sphere of the Great Mother. This sphere is also associated with the first mother of humanity, EVE, whose number value is 19 (ChVH), the number of circles used to construct the Cube of Space.

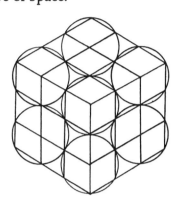

Figure 18
The generation of the Magic Cubes of the Tree of Life

This could be a good place to stop; however, there is more. When this cycle is continued, adding two more layers of circles, we create the Magic Square of Jupiter, the 4th sphere on the Tree of Life. The integrity of the Cube is maintained as it is expanded into its next level of expression. As this cycle goes further, the Magic Squares of Mars with 25 cells, and the Sun with 36 cells are inscribed, along with the remaining 4 Sephiroth. Of the Ten Sephiroth, nine of the cubic expressions are shown in Figure 19, Kether to Yesod

Figure 19
The Nesting of Magic Squares

All of these Magic Squares have one common central circle and point. They contain the intelligence of the Sephiroth or cube that precedes it, and are contained within the Sephiroth or cube, which succeeds it. Furthermore, if the focus went inward, the cubes of Chockmah and Kether can be seen.

If any of the diagonals of the cubes were connected from any direction, or any of the lines of the circles followed, many Trees of Life and many Cubes of Space would be seen. In fact, each circle contains a Cube of Space, and a Tree of Life. Each of these tiny trees contains at least 4 cubes, and each tiny cube contains 5 trees, one on each corner, and one at the center. The closest image to this idea was printed in Frater Achads, *The Anatomy Of The Body Of God,* in "The Macrocosmic Snow Flake."

Figure 20
The Microcosmic Snowflake

There is another diagram from the same book that shows a similar generation of the tree.

Figure 21

In the city of Abidos, Egypt, there is a temple dedicated to Osiris. On the portal of the temple is the symbol of the six-petaled flower, just described. It is at this location, legend says, that Isis brought together the mutilated body of Osiris and through the power of love, brought him back to life. For one night, they laid together and from that union came forth their Son, Horus. The twelve pieces of Osiris' body are representative of the sphere of Chockmah, sphere of the zodiac, and sphere of potential. Through the power of limitation, Isis was able to bring together the potential of Osiris and create their son, Horus.

FOOTNOTES

[1] *Secret Symbols of the Rosicrucians of the 16th and 17th Centuries.* Supreme Grand Lodge of AMORC, Inc.

[2] *The Book of Tokens,* by Dr. Paul Foster Case.

[3] Idea expanded from *A Practical Guide to Qabalistic Symbolism,* Gareth Knight, p.55, fig. 4b.

[4] Idea received during a presentation by David Tressemer and Roger Klarl on Sacred Geometry in Boulder, Colorado, February 1990.

[5] *The Sepher Yetzirah,* by Carlo Suares, p. 90. *TOL 7:6* by Dr. Case.

[6] *The Book of Tokens,* by Dr. Paul Foster Case

[7] *Sepher Yetzirah;* 1:1

[8] *TF;* 34:1, by Dr. Paul Foster Case.

[9] This formula was derived by Elizabeth Ordell, from Boulder, Colorado.

[10] Idea elaborated from *The Tarot of the Bohemians,* by Papus; Arcanum Books, 1958.

[11] *The Tarot of The Bohemians* by Papus.

[12] *The Philosophers of Nature.* Course on Spagyrics, Lesson 20.

[13] *TI;* 11:1, by Dr. Paul Foster Case.

[14] Idea expanded from the diagram of *A Key to the Cosmos and Numbers,* from *The Tarot,* by Dr. Paul Foster Case.

CHAPTER THREE

THE TREE AND THE CUBE

ost students of Qabalah are satisfied to leave the Cube as a mystical device, which is accessible through inner experience, turn their focus on the Tree of Life, and begin to label its parts in a way that helps them approach the path of return. With the help of dozens of books now available, we are able to study the Tree in many ways.

Dr. Paul Foster Case, well-known author of texts on the Hermetic Science, said, "In the study of the Qabalah there is no more important glyph than the Cube of Space, with perhaps the exception of the Tree of Life."[1]

When working with both forms, one will discover that there really is no separation; like seed and plant, they are forever joined and continually generate each other.

After taking a close look at the Cube, and breaking it down into its component parts, the Tree will quickly become apparent. The same applies to the Tree; the Cube will appear as we look at the different parts of the Tree.

Before embarking on the reconciliation of the Tree and the Cube, it is necessary to keep one special rule in mind. This rule is stated in the Sepher Yetzirah and can be summed up in the Number Ten. In Chapter I, we have quoted the Second through the Ninth Verses, which begin by referring to the Ten ineffable Sephiroth. The Fourth Verse leaves no room for question about just how many spheres there are:

> Ten is the number of the ineffable Sephiroth, ten and not nine, ten and not eleven. Understand this wisdom, and be wise by the perception. Search out concerning it, restore the Word to its Creator, and replace Him who formed it upon His throne.

The first attempts to bring the Tree and the Cube together were met with great difficulty. Every time an attempt was made, there seemed to be either eleven or nine spheres instead of ten. It became necessary to refer back to this Verse time and time again.

In Chapter 1:12, it is also clear that the Cube is generated from the Tree.

> Behold! From the Ten ineffable Sephiroth do proceed— the One Spirit of the Gods of the living, Air, Water, Fire; and also Height, Depth, East, West, South and North.

These boundaries establish the dimensions of the Cube of Space through the movement of the Mother letters from the center outward.

One of the first stumbling blocks to encounter is the sphere of Daath. It is crying to be included in the Ten Sephiroth; yet if it is, we would then have eleven spheres. If the sphere of the Moon, the foundation, is placed at the bottom of the Cube, where the Moon is assigned, the sphere of Malkuth is cut off and there are then nine. Ten and not nine, ten and not eleven is the rule that must be followed in understanding these two glyphs. The union of the Tree of Life and the Cube of Space becomes more apparent when these two glyphs are looked at from a three dimensional perspective instead of a two dimensional one. Trying to describe a three dimensional object from a two dimensional perspective is like trying to fit a round peg into a square hole. Frater Achad used a three dimensional model of the Tree of Life in *The Anatomy of The Body of God,* and Robert Wang used this three dimensional model in *The Qabalistic Tarot.* This model greatly enhances one's ability to grasp the proportions of the Tree.

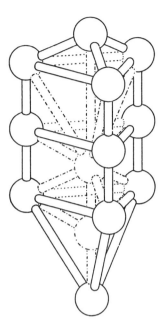

Figure 1[2]
The Three-Dimensional Tree

The particular models used in these two books do not reconcile the relationship between the Tree of Life and the Cube of Space.
It was not until working with solid geometrical forms that it became
apparent what was necessary to bring these two forms together.

THE OCTAHEDRON

The solid form of the Cube has within it an energy field. The
lines of this field are seen when the forces, centered on each face of the
Cube, which originate at the center of the Cube, are activated by the
three Mother letters (see page 25 of Chapter 1.) and are joined together.
It is these three Mother letters that establish the six faces of the Cube.
If we were to take the center of each face of the Cube and connect it
with every other face of the Cube, three squares would be formed,
each on a different plane. This form is called the octahedron. The
points of the octahedron are the same as the six permutations of the
name Jah, as this Divine Being projected himself from the center and
sealed the six directions. Each point of the octahedron comes to rest at
the exact center of the face of the Cube in which it lies. These points
are also the center of each Magic Square, which is represented by the
formative letter Heh when using the numbers from 1-9. The following
diagram shows the octahedron, and the three squares interwoven:

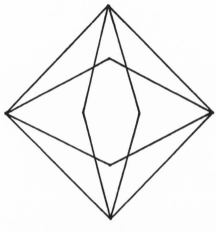

Figure 2
The Octahedron

The next thing to consider regarding the octahedron is that each point has a planetary attribution. It is also important to point out that at the center of the octahedron, we find the same three medians crossing as we do in the Cube. Each of the three squares is related to one of the three **Mother** letters that emanate their influence from the center. Aleph connects the above to the below, Mem the east and the west, and Sheen to the north and the south, as shown in the following diagram.

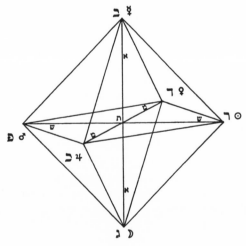

Figure 3
Planetary and letter placement on the points of the Octahedron

When bringing the Tree and the Cube together, it is necessary to consider the planetary attributions of the spheres of the Tree of Life and the faces of the Cube. From a nuts and bolts approach, both the Cube and the Tree have places allocated to the seven sacred planets known to the ancients. The task then is to place the Cube in the Tree or the Tree in the Cube and see if they fit in a way that rings true.

Since Verse 12 of the Sepher Yetzirah states that the six directions proceed from the Ten ineffable Sephiroth, the first union will be the Cube within the Tree. The same principle applies to the Cube as to the descent of the hexagram discussed in Chapter Two. It has its own process of condensation, beginning in the Ayin Soph Aur and proceeding into manifestation in the world of Assiah.

The following diagram shows the Tree with the condensation of the Cube. Notice that the upper face of the Cube, at the top of the Tree, is descending from the Ayin Soph Aur, and is bounded by the Supernal Triad, Kether, Chockmah, and Binah. The fourth corner is attributed to Daath. The bottom face of the Cube, which descends from the Ayin Soph Aur, is the top face of the Cube that moves from the archetypal world into the creative world.

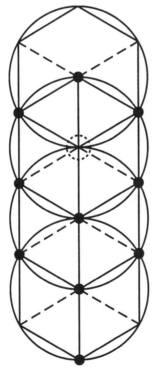

Figure 4
The descent of The Cube of Space on the Tree of Life

The movement of the Cube from one world to the next is completed by the bottom face of the above Cube. The bottom face becomes the upper face of the Cube beneath it and brings the energies of that which is above to that which is below. Notice that each above and below face are contained within a vesica, which marks the transition from one world to another. Just as the subconscious mind reflects the self-conscious mind, the Supernal Triad reflects the Ayin Soph Aur. This same reflection continues all the way down the Tree to the world of Assiah. As above, so below.

Within the framework of the Tree, four cubes can be seen. When Chapter One referred to the diagram of the macrocosmic cube, the Tree was seen in the Cube. Later, it will be shown that there are several Trees within the Cube. The relationship continues whether the pattern is expanded to the Macrocosm or contracted to the smallest fraction imaginable. This is the first basic relationship between the Cube and the Tree. One creates the other. One leads to the understanding of the other, and that **Understanding** is defined through the sphere of Binah.

On each corner of the Cube there is a Tree of Life. In the interior of the Cube, there is the combined energy of the Tree that brings the Holy Influence outward to the four corners. Seeking the source of this influence is the point of the study of the Cube.

All cubes have an octahedron within them. In taking a closer look at the Tree, it becomes clear that this third of the plutonic solids is none other than the Tree of Life.

Before trying to pigeonhole the Tree into the Cube, let us remember the source of both of these forms:

1. Six circles are tangent to a central seventh.

2. Twelve spheres are tangent to a central thirteenth.

3. It is the circle or sphere that encompasses each of these forms.

4. The circle or sphere is symbolic of pure Spirit.

5. The Cube is symbolic of Spirit as it creates a **Space** within the chaos for the sake of manifestation.

Descent on the Tree is the process of the involution of spirit where it condenses into the Cube of Space/Form. The Spirit is the seed (or pure possibility), the Tree is the germination, and the Cube is the fruit.

The relationship between the Tree and the Cube reminds us that all things are from One and have their birth from this source by adaptation. Even in the manifested state, the central idea is the same and the manifested object is created from the central idea, as seen in Figure 18 of Chapter 2. Looking at the octahedron is looking at the central idea as it exists at the heart of creation.

THE INVISIBLE PATHS

Those who have gone beyond a superficial observation of the Tree have learned of the sixteen invisible paths. We will now examine those paths to learn how they establish a relationship with the Tree and Cube. The following diagram shows the sixteen invisible paths.

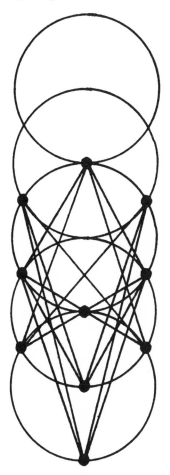

Figure 5
The Invisible Paths on the Tree of Life

In addition to the octahedron, the unicursal hexagram is formed. This structure can be inscribed over and over again without lifting the pencil from the paper. Thus, it represents the infinite ways in which the divine manifests itself in involutional and evolutional directions. The unicursal hexagram is inscribed on the Tree in the same place as the traditional hexagram, but is more fluid in its appearance. It can also be seen in a three-dimensional form by viewing the octahedron from a particular angle.[3]

Figure 6
The Unicursal Hexagram

When the octahedron is taken as the Tree of Life, placement of the Tree becomes more obvious. The following diagram shows the octahedron with the planetary attributions as they are inscribed on the Cube of Space:

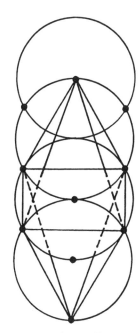

Figure 7
The Octahedron inscribed on the Tree of Life

At this point, the observant reader may decide to cast a few stones in this direction. It is obvious that there are a few changes on he Tree. One might think that there is a bit of stretching going on and that this explanation is no better than any other that has come forth in the past two thousand years. However, we find that this system is absolutely sound when we consider certain alchemical texts.

In the **Great Work**, to which every true hermetic student is committed, there is the task of transmuting base metals into gold and silver. This work is accomplished through the aid of the philosophical mercury. "**The Work of the Sun and the Moon is performed by the aid of Mercury.**"

On the above face of the Cube, we have the attribution of Beth, Key 1, The Magician, who is given the name Mercury, and is also under the influence of that same planet. Philosophical mercury represents superconsciousness, which on the Tree of Life is Kether. This is the power that the Magician draws down from above. He is the agent that "earths" it. "Its power is reborn if it be turned into Earth," according to *The Emerald Tablet.* The higher octave of the planet Mercury is Uranus, and it is attributed to the Mother letter Aleph, which is also attributed to superconsciousness. This is the first path that descends from Kether, where Mezla, the Holy Influence, descends into our sphere of awareness.

Dropping to the sphere of Tiphareth on the octahedron, which is traditionally the sphere of the Sun, the letter Tav and the planet Saturn are placed. The Sun is gold; Saturn is lead. The Great Work is the transmutation of lead into gold. Here, we can see that there is a direct connection between Saturn and the Sun, for the sphere of Saturn, whose number is three and has a root value of six, 1+2+3=6, reflects the sphere of the Sun, whose number is six and whose root value is three, 1+2+3+4+5+6=21, 2+1=3. There will be more explanation concerning the relationship between Binah and Tiphareth later on in this chapter as we consider the spheres of Chockmah and Binah and their placement on the octahedron.

On this model of the Tree, the sphere of Hod is given the attribution of the Sun instead of Mercury. Because Mercury is placed at the top of the Tree as well as on the above face of the Cube, something else must be placed here. It is not by process of elimination that the Sun is placed in the sphere of Hod. If we take the Briatic attributions of sound and color into consideration, we find the sphere of Hod receives the note 'D' natural, and the color orange. This is the color and sound given to the letter Resh, and these are assigned to the Sun, which has been placed in the sphere of Hod. Furthermore, the sphere of the Sun, Tiphareth, is colored yellow and receives the note 'E' natural. This is the sound and color attributed to Mercury.

In the Vedic symbol system of Tattwas, Hod, the sphere of Mercury, receives the Solar Tattwa, Tejas Pritivi, while the sphere of Tiphareth receives the Mercury Tattwa, Pritivi Pritivi. The letter Vav, which is associated with the Sphere of Tiphareth, also carries the same Tattwa as the letter Resh, and shows its influence in the sphere of Hod, as does Key 19 The Sun.[4]

Furthermore, the Golden Dawn places the Archangel Raphael in the sphere of Tiphareth, and Raphael is the Angel of Mercury. The Archangel Michael is placed in the sphere of Hod and Michael is the Angel of the Sun. Even in exoteric science, there is a strong connection between the gold (Au) of Tiphareth, and the mercury (Hg) of Hod. On the **Periodic Table of the Elements,** the atomic number of mercury is 80, and gold 79. They differ by a number of one. All of these exchanges between these two spheres add up to an obvious conclusion when dealing with the Tree and the Cube, and that is addressed by placing the Sun in Hod.

There is one final point concerning the relationship of Mercury, the Sun, and Saturn. It is in the sphere of Binah where the secret powers of the Life Force open up to the manifested universe. Descending from Binah to Tiphareth is the path of Zain, the path attributed to the sign of Gemini, where the planet Mercury is ruler. Also, notice that it is Key 1, The Magician, that first energized Binah from Kether. This path also sends its influence to Tiphareth through the path of Zain.

The final switch in the model of the octahedron is the sphere of the Moon and the sphere of Earth. These are Yesod and Malkuth. In this form, the sphere of the Moon, Yesod, is found in the position of Malkuth. If one takes into consideration that on the Tree of Life, the sphere of Yesod, the Moon, is called the Foundation, then it seems to be a fitting placement. It is the place where the Prima Materia gives birth to the concretized form. Its number is nine, the square of the sphere of Binah, which completes the numerical sequence of 1 through 9. On the Cube of Space, the Moon is placed at the below face just as Mercury is placed on the above face. (When addressing this form as a two-dimensional picture, it creates an illusion and can be confusing.) When Yesod is placed on the lowest point on the octahedron, it coincides with the planetary placements on the Cube of Space. When placing the Tree in the Cube in the form of the octahedron, the upper and lower mental planes exist on the same level simultaneously, under the direction of Tiphareth. These are Chesed, Geburah, Tiphareth, Netzach, and Hod. This places four planetary spheres in their respective faces on the Cube with Tiphareth in the center.

In the *Seven Rays of The QBL,* Frater Albertus says,

> "The basic structural pattern of the Tree of Life
> with its ten sephiroth has not been subjected to
> any significant changes. It practically has re-
> mained unchanged since its reputed compiler
> Moses de Leon, first wrote it down in the twelfth
> century. As with many other orthodox theories,
> sentimentality and other factors have also pre-
> vented necessary modifications in this system.
> Therefore, revisions have not only become nec-
> essary but absolutely essential.[5]

Here Frater Albertus speaks of the need to look beyond old conceptions and forms and examine the possibilities for new ones, so that the Qabalah and its students may grow.

When one applies the alchemical model of the transmutation of base metals into gold, the use of the octahedron makes perfect sense. An alchemical text, *The Generation of Gold,* by Admiraled, states,

> All things in the mineral kingdom aspire to be
> Gold. It is the destiny of each to become this,
> and through nature it will happen in her own
> good time, yet through art, if we learn her se-
> crets, and accelerate her process, we can bring
> about a rapid evolution.

When the transmutation is completed, all exist as one metal, gold. The same is true for humanity. All inwardly aspire to be one with the central Ego in Tiphareth, as we transmute our personalities from lead to gold. Here memory, will, desire, and intellect, express the **Mediating Influence** of the Central Ego, seated in Tiphareth, which reflects the One Self seated in Kether.

Like the paths of the Tree, the faces of the Cube must be traversed to gain in the experiences that lead to illumination. It is through the influence of the boundaries of the faces of the Cube that this takes place. Each face must be integrated, there are no exceptions. When this process is completed the Father and the Son are truly one, for Tiphareth, the Sun, which exists in the center of the Cube, radiates the will and influence of the Father. The following diagram shows the radiation from the center of the octahedron as it exists in the Cube of Space.

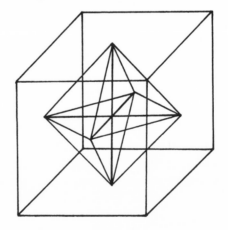

Figure 8
The Octahedron within the Cube of Space

There are now seven sacred planets placed on the Cube in relation to the Tree. Mercury, Moon, Venus, Jupiter, Mars, Sun, and Saturn. These are Kether, Yesod, Netzach, Chesed, Geburah, Hod, and
Tiphareth, respectively. Seven spheres? This could incite the voices
of rabbis, qabalists and hermetic students of the past two thousands
of years in joining in reprimand:

TEN AND NOT NINE, TEN AND NOT
ELEVEN, AND MOST CERTAIN OF ALL,
TEN AND NOT SEVEN.

We need to beware of excessive rationalization. An example of
this would be extending 7 to 28, then adding 2+8=10; this won't quite
do as there are three more spheres to deal with: Chockmah, Binah,
and Malkuth. Like anyone else who has tried to place the Tree in the
Cube, there is the illusion of running into a brick wall. The key to
this mystery lies in the eleventh and twelfth paths on the Tree. These
paths are related to the central axis of the octahedron, which extends
from the center to the above and below faces of the Cube.

The idea that the Macrocosmic Cube is actually a sphere of
operation of the Divine Mind also sheds some light on the placement of the last three Sephiroth. Since the microcosm is a model of
the Macrocosm, it, too, is a sphere of operation.

When looking at the points of the octahedron, the spheres of
Chockmah and Binah are not included. This is because they rest
outside the invisible paths that lead from Kether to Geburah, Kether
to Chesed, Kether to Netzach, and Kether to Hod. Their influence,
however, is most present. If readers will consider the two paths
leading from Kether to Chockmah and Binah, which are the paths of
Aleph and Beth, they will see that the same influences are located
on the above face of the Cube in the letter Beth, and the central axis
that connects the above to the below through the path of Aleph. The
expression of Chockmah and Binah can be found then on the central
axis. Considerations that point to this are the fourteenth path of
Daleth, the nineteenth path of Teth, and the twenty-seventh path of
Peh. They are the transverse paths that continually oscillate back
and forth between the Pillar of Mercy and the Pillar of Severity.

What is the purpose of these paths? They bring balance to the
spheres of Chockmah and Binah, Chesed and Geburah, and Netzach
and Hod. Where do the energies of these six Sephiroth rest when
they are brought into balance? On the Middle Pillar. This is the path
of the Uniting Intelligence, attributed to Key Two, the High Priestess,

and the letter Gimel. Now Chockmah is Wisdom and the value of Chockmah is seventy-three (ChKMH), the same value as the letter of Gimel (GML) when it is spelt in full. Also it is stated in the Psalms, "Speak unto thy sister Wisdom" (Chockmah).

When one takes nine circles of equal diameter and starts with the sphere of Kether and ends in the traditional placement of the sphere of Malkuth, each of these nine spheres will fit along the Middle Pillar, tangent to the one that precedes it and follows it.[6]

The following diagram shows the first nine spheres on the Middle Pillar. As this occurs, there is a movement of the spheres, and Yesod ends up in the place of Malkuth and becomes the Foundation of the Tree of Life. This is its rightful place since the foundation is always placed at the bottom to support **The House**, and Beth, meaning "house", is located on the above face of the Cube.

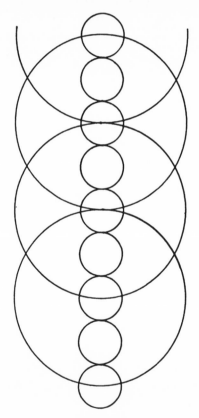

Figure 9
The Sephiroth balanced on the Middle Pillar

Another reason to place Chockmah and Binah on the central axis is that alchemically, Chockmah is the principle of sulphur and the seat of the Life Force, Fire. Binah is the principle of salt and the element of Earth. She is also the Prima Materia which is attributed to the element of Water. Now, the roots of Fire and Water emanate from the center under the letters, Sheen and Mem. Sheen connects the north and the south and Mem connects the east and west, with Tav residing at the center. Now Jah seals the six directions from the center with the three letters (IHV) and Yod is Chockmah, Heh is Binah, and Vav is Tiphareth. This brings us back to the concept that the Father and the Mother and the Son are **One.**

The following diagram shows the three alchemical principles as they are inscribed upon the Tree of Life.

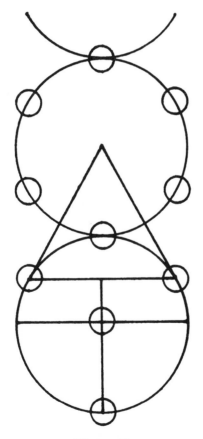

Figure 10
The Three Alchemical Principles on the Tree of LIfe

Thus far, nine of the ten spheres have been placed upon the octahedron within the structure of the Cube. The Tree and the Cube are almost reconciled. The tenth sphere, Malkuth, is the final consideration. Since Yesod displaced Malkuth from its traditional placement, it would seem that Malkuth is a fugitive and, in one sense, it is. However, take a good look at the traditional two-dimensional glyph of the Tree. At the bottom of the Tree, we find the sphere of Malkuth. Notice how the three paths that descend from Yesod, Hod, and Netzach all converge to form the apex of a downward pointing triangle. The sphere Malkuth is like a vessel that is receiving the waters of creation. The triangle is like a funnel that focuses the descending energies into its vessel. The following diagram shows the vessel being filled by the Holy Influence that descends from above.

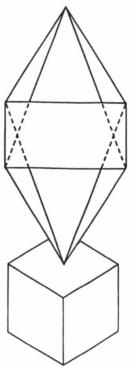

Figure 11
The Tree of Life filling the Vessel of Malkuth

Since each individual is a microcosmic expression of the Macrocosm, in a sense we are vessels like the Cube of Space. The idea that the intelligences of the Tree of Life converge into a vessel,

named Malkuth, in the form of the Cube of Space, fits with the esoteric doctrine that says:

> "There is a focusing of a "Ray" of the fiery Life-
> Breath of the One Identity within the personal
> organism."7

This personal organism is a vessel which receives the impact
from that which is above.

Kether is the recipient of the influence streaming from the
Ayin Soph Aur. It receives that influence but is separated from it by
the Negative Veils of the Absolute; so, Malkuth receives the influence of the Tree of Life. Kether is in Malkuth and Malkuth is in
Kether, but in a different manner. Once again, as above so below.

Malkuth is separated in appearance from the main body of
the Tree, like Kether is apparently separated from the Negative Veils.
The reality is that the intelligence dwells within the vessel, and
awaits the moment when it is fully released and in full control over
the vessel in which it is contained. Malkuth and hence, the Cube of
Space, is the fruit of the Tree and, like an apple and its seeds, contains the "intelligence" or structural code of the Tree from which it
FALLS. When the apple falls to Earth it is apparently separated from
the tree, yet it is continually guided by the germinating influence
that dwells within. Malkuth contains within its center the limited
spectrum of name and form. All the influence that is above is neatly
tucked away at its core, seed, or center. To consciously access the influence (Mezla) and to germinate the seed that teaches the secrets of
our Divine Beingness is our task. That is why the sages tell us to
seek the ways of Nature and she will reveal her secrets. In order to
access this information of the seed, one must be in harmony with
the Mind of the All, as it expresses itself in the ways of nature.

Returning to the Macrocosmic model of the cube and viewing
it as a sphere, we can see that the principle of correspondence also applies to the microcosmic cube. The Macrocosm contains the Tree and
so does the microcosm. The Tree dwells within the Cube as well as
makes up its exterior structure. The twelve spheres tangent to a central thirteenth sphere are a unifying principle, whether dealing with
Macrocosm or microcosm. It is the thirteenth path of the Tree of Life
that speaks to this unity; for unity (AChD) and love (AHBH) have the
value of thirteen and represent the balancing force in the universe.

We have yet another example of the Cube as the sphere of
Malkuth. When a line is drawn connecting the four corners of the

Cube we, have a horizontal square. Within the center of each of these lines, we find the cardinal points of the octahedron, which define the planetary positions of Venus, Mars, Jupiter, and the Sun, on the east, north, west and south faces. If the lines of this horizontal square of the octahedron are bisected, another square would be formed, which would be the square root of the square formed on the surface of the Cube. This process of bisecting these squares can go on infinitely.

The next step is to connect the point of one of the exterior corners and proceed inward, touching the corner of each square. As the points are connected, a spiral, which is the signature of Kether, the beginning of the whirlings, is formed. The act of intention is still continuing within the sphere of Malkuth, for it must and will become the Bride of the Most High God, and the Kether of the next Tree.

The following diagram shows the faces of the various cubes and octahedrons as the spiral travels towards the center.

Figure 12
The spiral formed by octahedrons within cubes, and cubes within octahedrons.

In alchemy, all things have within them the three Principles, Mercury, Sulphur, and Salt. In the process of calcination the material to be worked upon is reduced to ash. When the ash is leached and washed, the principle of salt is revealed. It is the principle of salt that defines one living thing from another. The salt of a fern is different from the salt of a yucca plant. When the Cube receives the specific act of intention from the spiral motion of Kether, it defines the nature that the specific cube will take. Even though the salt of a fern and of a yucca plant can be reduced to a common inorganic compound, that is predominantly potassium carbonate, the way in which these salts behave is different; they contain the specific intelligence of the creative intention that originated in Kether.

If we look to the sphere of Saturn and its Magic Square, we will see how the Tree of Life is formed on the boundaries of the Cube. Remember that the Tree and the Cube are forms within a sphere: they always have a spheroid quality no matter what the outward appearance may be. The following diagram illustrates the placement of the Tree of Life on the boundaries of the Cube of Space.

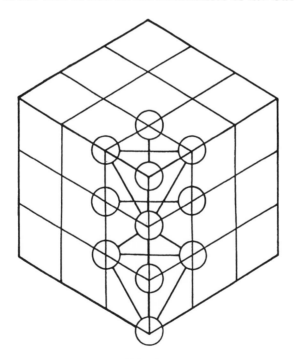

Figure 13
The Tree of Life on the corners of the Cube of Space

Since the Tree and the Cube have a spheroid quality, one must conclude that the Tree, seen in Figure 13, also curves when it is placed upon a sphere. In the picture of the Cube, it is not so obvious that there is a Tree on each corner. By simply turning the Cube from side to side, it reveals the different Trees that exist on its boundaries.

There are some profound points that come to light when we consider:

1. The four diagonals in relationship to the Malkuth of each Tree. There is a Tree on each corner, northeast, northwest, southeast, and southwest. The aspirant may access the different Trees through the four diagonals.

2. On each below corner, a diagonal ascends from Malkuth, through the center of the Cube, and reaches Daath at the above corner on the Tree of Life, which is diagonally opposite it.

As each below corner is the sphere of Malkuth, each above corner is the invisible sphere of Daath. As there are four worlds in the Qabalah which can be identified with the elements Atziluth-fire, Briah-water, Yetzirah-air, and Assiah-earth, there are four Trees visible on the Cube which have their specific elemental quality. The northeast corner is cardinal Fire through the sign of Aries, the southwest corner is fixed Water of Scorpio, the northwest corner is cardinal Air of Libra, and the southeast corner is fixed Earth of Taurus. Figure 14 shows a diagonal as it ascends from the sphere of Malkuth to the sphere of Daath.

In *Genesis* 3:5-6, the serpent said to Eve, "God knows in fact that on the day you eat it your eyes will be opened and you will be like gods, knowing good and evil."

The fall from innocence took place after **KNOWLEDGE** (Daath) was experienced. In the *Sepher Yetzirah*, Chapter 1:5, we read, "The Ten ineffable Sephiroth have ten vast regions bound unto them; boundless in origin and having no ending; an abyss of good and ill..." It was eating from the tree of knowledge of "good and evil" that set the fall into motion. Adam and Eve were to sense their godliness, yet they were unable to use their Divine Power due to lack of experience. On the Tree of Life, Daath sits by the Abyss of Good and Evil. It is the line of demarcation between the Supernal Triad that remains forever undefiled, and the world of personal experience which is subject to the illusion of name and form.

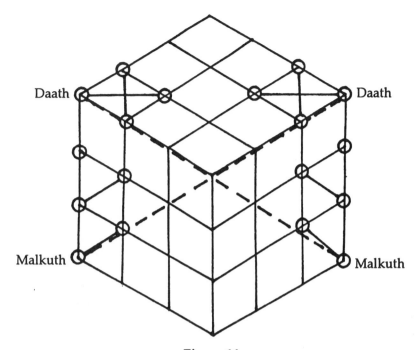

Figure 14
The Diagonals extending from Malkuth to Daath

The consequence of the fall brought the sphere of Daath down to the place of Malkuth.[8]

Many thoughts may come to mind when one examines the points where the spheres of the Tree are inscribed. First of all, the trees are defined by the crossing of the lines that form the Magic Square of Saturn. It is through the process of separation that the One Life creates. It is also through the power of the Knowledge of Good and Evil that allows the experience of separation and, thus, the illusion of being cut off from our divine parents.

The word for Evil (RO) has a value of 270. The value of INRI, the sentence nailed on the cross of Jesus when he was crucified, is also 270. The product of 6x45 is 270, which is the total value of the six faces of the Cube of Space, when the numbers of the Magic Square of Saturn are used, 1 through 9.

As the four Malkuths, located on the below corners ascend through the center of the Cube and arrive at the sphere of Daath, integration of the entire Cube of Space is possible. The final diagonal to be traversed in alphabetical and numerical order is final Tzaddi. Now Daath has a value of 406, when it is spelled DAATh.⁹ The value of Malkuth is 496. When final Tzaddi is traversed, it brings forth its value of 90 to that of the 406 of DAATh and equals the value of Malkuth returning the Creator to his throne. Tav, when spelled in full (ThV), has a value of 406. Tav is the letter located in the center of the Cube. When the **Fall** from the garden took place, that which was created in the image and likeness of God, humanity, became **People of the Earth.** They were **Divided** from their birth-right as children of the Most High until they learned the secret of the **Cross**—in this case the Gnostic Cross of the Cube of Space. Upon the integration of this cross, they would experience their true nature, as Divine Beings.

Genesis 1:1, "In the beginning the creative power of the Life Breath separated the Heavens from the Earth," speaks of this power to divide itself in order to express itself. Thus, we have the ten aspects of Divine beingness as expressed by the Ten ineffable Sephiroth.

By carrying this idea of separation a little further, we can see that there are fifty-six crossings on the surface of the Cube. This allows placement of the Minor Arcana of the Tarot on the Boundaries of the Cube of Space. Placement of the Major Arcana has already been established by the letters of the Hebrew alphabet. The Minor Arcana is actually the interaction of the wanderers, the seven sacred planets, and the Holy Influence, Mezla, which streams from the stars or constellations that represent the twelve simple letters that make up the twelve boundaries of the Cube.

FOOTNOTES

TF, by Dr. Paul Foster Case.

The Anatomy of the Body Of God, by Frater Achad, page 64, plate "C".

When the octahedron is tilted and the observer looks into its center, a three dimensional unicursal hexagram is seen. Information on the unicursal hexagram can be found in TL, by Dr. Case, *The Qabalistic Tarot*, by Robert Wang, and *777* by Aleister Crowley.

SC; 9:2, and *OT;* 10:3 by Dr. Paul Foster Case. In *OT;* 10:3, Dr. Case refers to Key 19 as representative of the sphere of Hod.

The Seven Rays of the QBL, by Frater Albertus. Samuel Weiser, 1980.

The nine circles are tangent on the middle pillar, from Kether to Yesod, when the spheres of the Tree of Life equals 1/4 the radius of the construction circles. *TL;* 7:6, by Dr. Paul Foster Case.

TF; 31:1, by Dr. Case

Idea from *The Ladder of Lights*, by William Gray.

The usual spelling of Daath is DOTh with the value of 474. "Aleph is often interchanged with H, or O; and generally these letters, as being very nearly allied in pronunciation, are very often interchanged". Gesenius, Hebrew-Chaldee Lexicon to the Old Testament.

CHAPTER FOUR

THE PLACEMENT OF THE MAJOR AND MINOR TRUMPS

he 22 Hebrew letters of the Chaldean Aleph-Beth have been placed around the boundaries of the Cube of Space. Many students of the Tarot are well aware of the correspondences of the Chaldean Aleph-Beth to the 22 Major Trumps. In Dr. Paul Foster Case's, *The Tarot, A Key to the Wisdom of the Ages*, we get the placement of the 22 letters and their corresponding Major Keys on the Cube of Space. He says in the chapter on the Emperor,

> "No more than hints of this cube symbolism can
> be given in this introductory text, but we have
> thought it best to include the figure of the Cube
> of Space, since careful study will reveal to dis-
> cerning readers many clues to a deeper under-
> standing of the Tarot symbolism."

With the exception of a few more details concerning the Cube in the lessons of the B.O.T.A., there is nothing more available about the Cube that the author is aware of. The following presentation will bring the reader up-to-date concerning the information available about the Cube of Space. The correspondences used are those from *The Tarot*, by Case.

The three Mother letters, Aleph, Mem, and Sheen, are Keys 0, 12, 20. They also correspond to the three supernal planets, Uranus, Neptune, and Pluto respectively. The line that extends from the center to the above, from the center to the below, is represented by Key 0, the Fool. Key 12, the Hanged Man, moves from the center to the east and from the center to the west. Key 20, Judgment, moves from the center to the north, and the center to the south. It is important to note that the energies manifested in the six faces of the Cube receive their creative impulse from the center of the Cube, through the vehicles of the three Mother letters. Refer to Figure 4 in Chapter 1.

The Tarot Keys corresponding to the six faces of the cube are:

Above, Key 1, The Magician
Below, Key 2, The High Priestess
These Keys are connected by Key 0, the Fool.

east, Key 3, The Empress
west, Key 10, The Wheel of Fortune
These keys are connected by Key 12, the Hanged Man.

south, Key 19, The Sun
north, Key 16, The Tower
These Keys are connected by Key 20, Judgement.

These six faces are, of course, six of the seven double letters. The seventh letter is represented by Key 21, The World, which rests in the center. The following diagram shows the seven Tarot Keys as they appear on the six faces, and the center.

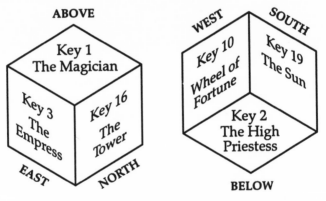

Figure 1
Placement of the Major Keys – Planetary

The twelve Keys, representing the twelve simple letters, are next in our considerations. These twelve Keys are positioned in the same place as the twelve zodiacal signs, as seen in Chapter 1, Figure

Key 4 – The Emperor, the northeast line.

Key 5 – The Hierophant, the southeast line.

Key 6 – The Lovers, the east above line.

Key 7 – The Chariot, the east below line.

Key 8 – Strength, the north above line.

Key 9 – The Hermit, the north below line.

Key 11 – Justice, the northwest line.

Key 13 – Death, the southwest line.

Key 14 – Temperance, the west above line.

Key 15 – The Devil, the west below line.

Key 17 – The Star, the south above line.

Key 18 – The Moon, the south below line.[1]

The following diagram shows the 12 zodiacal Keys around the 12 boundary lines of the Cube of Space.

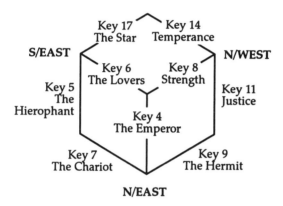

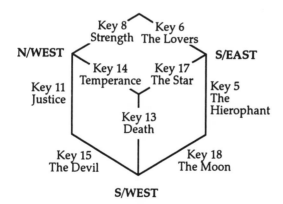

Figure 2
Placement of the Major Keys – Zodiacal

There are several systems that can be placed around these faces and lines. In fact, you can use any of the different languages you choose to understand the Cube, whether it is Letters, Tarot Keys, Sound, Color, Tattwas, Numbers, or, perhaps, other correspondences not considered here.

The final attributions are the four diagonals shown in Chapter 1, Figure 12. The Tarot Keys associated with the Final letters and the diagonals, are the same as those placed on the faces and lines, under the same letter name. Final Kaph is The Wheel of Fortune Key, 10, Final Mem is The Hanged Man, Key 12, Final Nun is Death, Key 13, Final Peh is The Tower, Key 16, and Final Tzaddi is The Star, Key 17.[2]

This is an update on the known available information on the Cube of Space. From this point on, some new ideas will be introduced. It is believed that this information will be welcomed by all students of the Tarot, who have been looking forward to an elaboration on the Cube of Space and its relationship to the Tarot and Tree of Life.

The Tarot not only contains the 22 Major Trumps, it also contains the 56 Minor Trumps (which are not so minor when one thinks about it). The power expressed by the symbolism of the Major Keys shows the specific ways the One Life operates through its centers of expression. The Minor Keys show an even greater expression of this power, for they join together the individual aspects of expression of the One, and bringing them together to create more complex vehicles which allow for more specific forms of expression. An example of the level of complexity which forms a specific vehicle of expression can be seen in an individual's astrological chart. **The letters, whose intelligence permeates the entire universe, find themselves fitting vehicles of expression through the zodiacal signs and planets of this world system.**[3] These influences make up a particular arrangement within the individual, and the code of expression is then manifested through that individual, as he develops in his ability to be self-consciously awake.

The forms expressed by the Minor Arcana are a model of the Great Wheel of the zodiac. Each of us, of course, has our own personal pattern which can be worked out separately from the Minor Arcana.

The Minor Keys are a packed symbol system, which speak to at least two and sometimes several Major Trumps or letters of the Chaldean Aleph-Beth.

The Tarot is perhaps the most important synthesized system of Qabalistic study ever to come into the possession of humanity. It's construction is based on the Law of Tetragrammaton,[4] using numbers, letters, and sounds.[5] A strong understanding of the symbols of the Tarot greatly assists the students in grasping their own personal transformation as they travel the paths of the Tree of Life, and the currents of the Cube of Space.

The placement of the Minor Trumps on the Cube of Space is accomplished by taking a few initial steps:

First, by using the limiting power of Saturn, the sphere of Binah. This is accomplished by taking the unlimited potential of Chockmah, limiting an aspect of it, and placing that idea in a vessel, the Cube, as did JAH, when he sealed the six directions.[6]

Second, by using the building block numbers 1,3,6,9. The Cube is One, for we are expressing the One Life, as it is emanating from the Crown of Primal Will, Kether, and how it bears the fruit of this One Will in the sphere of Malkuth, the tenth sphere.

The Cube is Three, because the trinity is always the means of expression of the One. As we take the influence of the sphere of Chockmah, as manifested by the twelve signs of the zodiac, we find a trinitarian expression in the three decanates of each sign. When each of the three planetary rulers, of the three decanates of a particular sign are connected together, they form a triangle within the Cube. Collectively, the 36 decanates inscribe the triangles which make up the octahedron within the Cube.

The Cube is Six by virtue of its six faces and how each sign is ruled by six major forces— three planets and three signs. For example, the decanates of Aries are ruled by Aries, Leo, and Sagittarius from the zodiacal points, and Mars, the Sun, and Venus from the planetary points.

The Cube is Nine, because of the nature of the Magic Square of Saturn. It is the Magic Square of Saturn that is the framework for the sphere of Malkuth and the Cube of Space. The value of the sphere of Saturn is 3 and its square is 9, 3x3=9.

The following diagram shows the sphere of Malkuth with the Magic Square of Saturn. Pay particular attention to the points that divide the nine cells. It is the **CROSSING** of these lines that create the points where the Minor Arcana are expressed. One of the older symbols for the letter Tav, the letter attributed to Saturn, is the cross. Once again, we see the limiting power of Saturn setting a space apart for the expression of the One Life as it divides itself, the One into the many.

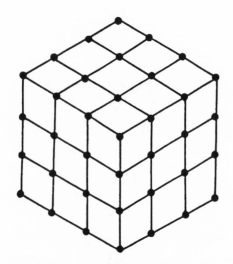

Figure 3
The Grid of the Magic Square of Saturn

It is on these points that the 36 Minor Keys, numbering 2-10, the 16 Court cards, made up of 4 Kings, 4 Queens, 4 Knights, and 4 Pages, and the 4 Aces are placed. These keys have been divided into three groups, for they represent different modes of expressing the combination of the various Major Keys.

The Keys numbering from 2-10 are the 36 decanates of the zodiacal wheel. Figure 4 gives a quick reference to the sequence of number, planet, and sign of the 36 decanates, as well as their placement in its particular world of the Qabalah, marked by the suit of each particular Minor Key.

Wands – ruling the world of Atziluth,
Cups – ruling the Briatic world,
Swords – ruling the world of Yetzirah,
Pentacles – ruling the world of Assiah.

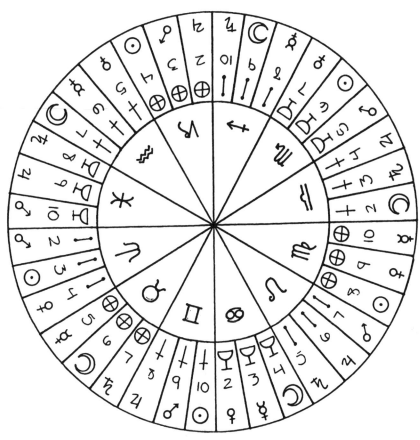

Figure 4[7]
The Great Zodiacal Wheel and the Chaldean order of the planets

The pattern of Figure 4 is then placed on the points of the Magic Square of Saturn, according to the zodiacal signs on the boundaries of the Cube.

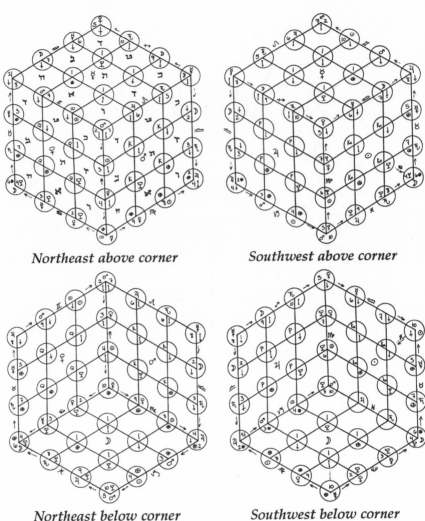

Northeast above corner   Southwest above corner

Northeast below corner   Southwest below corner

Figure 5
The Minor Arcana on the Cube of Space
through the Magic Square of Saturn

It is here that a decision must be made concerning the particular order of planets that will be used in this work. There are several planetary orders. One example is the days of the week. Monday (Moon), Tuesday (Mars), Wednesday (Mercury), Thursday (Jupiter), Friday (Venus), Saturday (Saturn), and Sunday, (the Sun).[8] The Chaldean order of the planets, is an order that follows the movement of the Sephiroth as the Mezla descends the Tree of Life. The descent of Mezla takes the form of a lightning bolt, as mentioned in Chapter

1:6 of the *Sepher Yetzirah,* "The Ten ineffable Sephiroth have the appearance of the Lightning Flash." Since the zodiacal year begins in the sign of Aries, the Chaldean order begins with the sphere of Geburah, attributed to the planet Mars, ruler of Aries. This sphere is chosen as the starting point instead of the planet Saturn, which is the first sphere on the Tree of Life to hold a planetary signature. The planetary order descends from the sphere of Mars to the sphere of the Sun, and continues an orderly descent through Venus and Mercury, terminating at the sphere of the Moon. The order continues at the sphere of Binah, the sphere of Saturn, and continues to descend the Tree in sephirotic order. This order repeats itself throughout the 36 decanates until the end of the year in the sign of Pisces, where the whole cycle begins once again in the sign of Aries.

The traditional planetary order is the order of elemental triplicities. These are the conventional astrological attributions to the 36 decanates. In this traditional system, each elemental sign is ruled by itself and the other two signs of that element. For example, Aries, a fire sign, has Aries as the ruler of the first decanate. The other two signs of that element are Leo and Sagittarius. The factor that determines which sign rules which decanate is in their order of appearance in the zodical year. Since Leo is the next fire sign to follow Aries, it is the ruler of the second decanate of Aries. Sagittarius is then the ruler of the third decanate, for it is the fire sign that follows Leo. When the three decanates of Leo are considered, the first decanate is ruled by Leo, the second by Sagittarius, which is once again the next fire sign in the series. The final decanate of Leo is ruled by Aries, which completes the circle of fire signs.[9]

Dr. Case used the elemental order in his writings. It is here that this work will deviate from that of Dr. Case. There are a few reasons for this. First, the Cube of Space is in direct relationship to the Tree of Life as stated in Chapter 1:12 of the *Sepher Yetzirah.* "Behold! From the Ten ineffable Sephiroth do proceed – (the above, below, north, south, east and west)." Since the Tree of Life is the matrix for the Cube, it seems proper to use sephirotic attributions for the points on the Cube rather than the elemental triplicities. Second, the potential for planetary expression is limited with this traditional order in that five of the seven planets are expressed six times, and two of the planets are expressed three times, leaving an imbalance. The following list shows the way in which the planets are expressed, in the traditional elemental order:

Fire

> Aries – Mars, Sun, Jupiter
> Leo – Sun, Jupiter, Mars
> Sagittarius – Jupiter, Mars, Sun

Earth

Taurus – Venus, Mercury, Saturn
Virgo – Mercury, Saturn, Venus
Capricorn – Saturn, Venus, Mercury

Air

Gemini – Mercury, Venus, Saturn +(Uranus)
Libra – Venus, Saturn +(Uranus), Mercury
Aquarius – Saturn+(Uranus), Mercury, Venus.

Water

Cancer – Moon, Mars, Jupiter+(Neptune)
Scorpio – Mars, Jupiter+(Neptune), Moon
Pisces – Jupiter+(Neptune), Moon, Mars

In employing this order, Mars, Jupiter, Venus, Mercury and Saturn are used six times. The Sun and Moon, are used three times. This poses an unequal distribution of planetary energy in relationship to the Tree of Life, and how it is expressed through the octahedron.

It is interesting to note what is revealed when one looks at the construction of the octahedron in relationship to the different orders of the planets. The following diagram shows the traditional order of the elementary triplicities, and how this order falls on the octahedron.

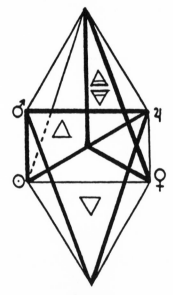

Figure 6
The Elemental Order of the Planets inscribed on the Octahedron

As you can see, the octahedron connects only three of the triangles and leaves many of the remaining lines unexpressed. The application of the Chaldean order of the planets will reveal a greater expression of the central energy of the Cube. The following diagram shows the Chaldean order of the planets, followed by a diagram which gives the placement of this order on the octahedron.

♂	☉	♀	☿	☽	♄	♃
2 | ♈	3 | ♈	4 | ♈	5 ⊕ ♉	6 ⊕ ♉	7 ⊕ ♉	8 † ♊
9 † ♊	10 † ♊	2 Y ♋	3 Y ♋	4 Y ♋	5 | ♌	6 | ♌
7 | ♌	8 ⊕ ♍	9 ⊕ ♍	10 ⊕ ♍	2 † ♎	3 † ♎	4 † ♎
5 Y ♏	6 Y ♏	7 Y ♏	8 | ♐	9 | ♐	10 | ♐	2 ⊕ ♑
3 ⊕ ♑	4 ⊕ ♑	5 † ♒	6 † ♒	7 † ♒	8 Y ♓	9 Y ♓
10 Y ♓						

Figure 7
The Chaldean Order of the planets

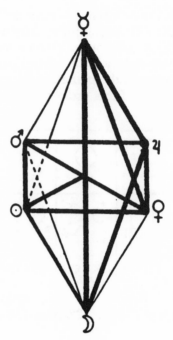

Figure 8
The Chaldean order inscribed on the Octahedron

This diagram shows a much greater expression of the planetary energies.

The reason for examining these different orders has to do with the message that each order has to offer as far as their expressing the various influences (Mezla) of the letters of the Aleph-Beth. The following chart shows the wheel of the zodiac with each of the two orders as they unfold throughout the zodiacal year. The Chaldean order is on the inner circle and the elemental order is on the outer circle.

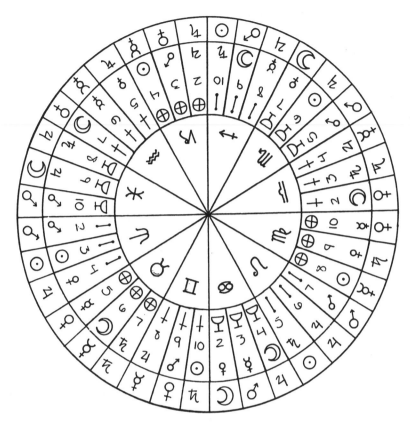

Figure 9
Chaldean and Elemental Order of the Planets on the Great Wheel

Either of these two orders can be used in this work; however, it would seem that the Chaldean order is more appropriate when working with the Cube.

We will begin the planetary associations with the points formed by the intersection of the vertical and horizontal lines of the Magic Square of Saturn. We will then place our attention on the lines attributed to the twelve zodiacal signs, which form the outer boundaries of the Cube, and follow the points that are inscribed on them. As a reference, a diagram of the Cube will be used to show the planetary and zodiacal influences as they flow on the exterior of the Cube, and at the same time a diagram of the octahedron will be used to show how these forces work within the structure of the Cube.

As the points on each zodiacal line are considered, the experience of these forces will be illuminated by a small paragraph using gematria to highlight the particular flow of energy.

The first three points under consideration are those of the sign of Aries, the beginning of the zodiacal year. They lie on the northeast line which descends from the above northeast corner to the below northeast corner. The planets within the three decanates are Mars the Sun, and Venus. The above point, which forms the northeast above corner, is attributed to Mars, and the 2 of Wands. The middle point is attributed to the Sun and the 3 of Wands, and the lower third point is given to Venus and the 4 of Wands.

The following diagram shows the planetary points on the northeast corner of Aries. The diagram of the octahedron reveals the triangle formed by connecting the faces of the Cube which are assigned the planetary signatures used in the three decanates of Aries, as expressed through the 2,3, and 4 of Wands. The faces connected are: the north-Mars, the south-Sun, and the east-Venus. We can see a horizontal triangle formed between the northern, southern, and eastern faces of the Cube. This triangle expresses the planetary influence of Aries.

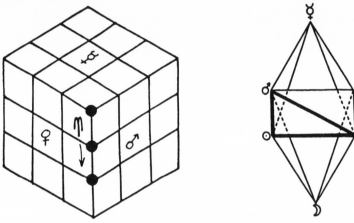

Figure 10
The placement of the 2, 3 and 4 of Wands

In the sign of Scorpio, we will find the same triangle formed on the octahedron as that in the sign of Aries. This is done through the agency of the 5, 6, 7 of Cups. If we refer to Figure 7, we will see that the same order repeats itself in the sign of Scorpio as that of the sign of Aries (Mars, Sun, Venus). Its placement on the Cube is the diametricly opposite corner, the southwest. It connects with the sign of Aries through Final Nun, the diagonal that ascends from the northeast below corner to the southwest above corner.

As the influence of Aries travels through the diagonal of Final Nun, aspirants are confronted with their fear of death. From this onfrontation, they learn that the Great Work **SHALL BE CONTINUED**, and at the **APPOINTED TIME, THE RIGHT HAND** f the One, shall **SUPPORT** them, and the **PERFECTION** of the **IMAGINATIVE INTELLIGENCE**, will bring forth the **KEY OF THE GREAT ART,** and deliver the **UNIVERSAL MEDICINE**, with **PEACE ROFOUND.**

ININ – Shall be continued.

MVOD – Moade – Appointed time.

IMINI – Yimini – The right hand.

SMK – Samek – Support.

MKLL – Miklahl – Perfection.

KMIVNI – Kamyuni – Imaginative.

Clavis Artis – Key of art.

Medicina Catholica – Universal medicine.

Pax Profunda – Peace Profound.

These words all have the value of 120, the value of the intelli-ence of the letter NUN, the Imaginative Intelligence.

The signs of Taurus/Sagittarius, Gemini/Capricorn, Can-er/Aquarius, and Leo/Pisces share a similar relationship as ries/Scorpio. These will be dealt with as they come up.

The next sign in the wheel is Taurus. The energy flows from he southeast below corner to the southeast above corner. The plane-ary points on this line are Mercury, the above point; Moon, the be-ow point; and Saturn, the middle point. The following diagram hows the influence of Taurus, and the place where its planetary ulers inscribe the central axis of the octahedron through the 5, 6, nd 7 of Pentacles.

Notice that in the sign of Taurus there is no triangle formed. 'here is a central line that extends from the above to the below, con-ecting Kether to Yesod via the middle pillar. Key 2, The High 'riestess, attributed to the Moon is exalted in the sign of Taurus. It is he Key attributed to the Uniting Intelligence, which connects Kether ɔ Tiphareth on the Middle Pillar. It is also interesting to note that ʿey 5, The Hierophant, the revealer of the mysteries, brings the in-ɔrmation from the below face of the subconscious mind to the ʿbove face of the self-conscious mind, represented by Key 1, The ʿagician.

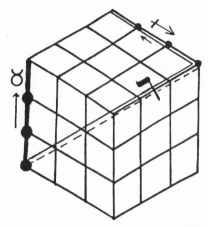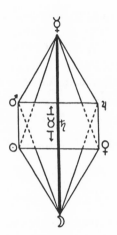

Figure 11
The placement of the 5, 6 and 7 of Pentacles

The letter Vav, assigned to Taurus, is attributed to Tiphareth and is the third letter of the Divine Name of IHV. Within this sign, Tarot Key 5 (the "Revealer of the Mysteries") and the letter Vav (the nail or hook) connects that which is above to that which is below through the agency of the Middle Pillar. There is one other sign which inscribes this same line: it is the sign of Sagittarius through the 8, 9, and 10 of Wands. On the traditional Tree of Life, Sagittarius continues the Middle Pillar from Tiphareth to Yesod. There are profound connections between these signs, for the letter Samek (whose value is 60) reduces to 6, the same value of the letter Vav. This letter is also that which sustains and supports, as does the foundation, Yesod. Key 14, Temperance is also the bridge between the animal soul, Nephesh, and the Central Ego in Tiphareth. Another connection is the number value of the Tarot keys: Key 14, when reduced to 1+4=5, corresponds to the value of Key 5, The Hierophant.[10]

Final Kaph, assigned to Jupiter, is the interior diagonal connecting the southeast below corner with the center. The diagonal moves from the center to the northwest above corner. This diagonal brings the influence of the letter Vav, and Key 5, the Revealer of the Mysteries, to bear on the currents of Key 14, Temperance. That which **Tests** Thee, also grants **The Vision of The Lord unto Thee,** so that Thou may **Behold** the **Swelling Majesty** of the **Law** of the **ONE,** and become energized by the projective quality of the **Nitre.**

BChN – Bakan – To try to test

MChZH – Makhazeh – The vision of the Lord be granted unto thee.

HNH – Hinnay – Behold.

GAVN – Gawawen – Swelling majesty

HLKH – Halahkah – Traditional law.

Nitre – Fiery alchemical salt.

All of these words have a value of 60, the value of Samek.

The third sign in the Great Zodiacal Wheel is Gemini. The planets ruling the decanates of Gemini are Jupiter moving from the southwest corner to the north, Mars ruling the middle point of the line of Gemini, and the Sun approaching the northeast above corner. The zodicial influence of Gemini ends before it hits the northeast intersection of Aries and Leo. The points of Gemini are expressed through the 8, 9 and 10 of Swords.

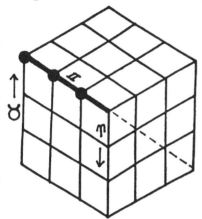 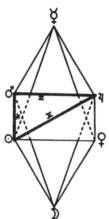

Figure 12
The placement of the 8, 9 and 10 of Swords

The sign of Gemini completes two cycles in the Tarot series. It completes the cycle of numbers, 2 through 10, and the first cycle of cardinal (Aries), fixed (Taurus), and mutable (Gemini) signs. It is interesting to note that all of the cardinal signs have the numbers 2, 3, 4. For example, cardinal fire is the 2, 3, 4 of Wands, cardinal water is the 2, 3, 4 of Cups, cardinal air is the 2, 3, 4 of Swords, and cardinal earth is the 2, 3, 4 of Pentacles. The fixed and mutable signs follow a similar pattern with the fixed signs being, 5, 6, 7, and the mutable signs have the numbers 8, 9, 10. The following chart shows this pattern.

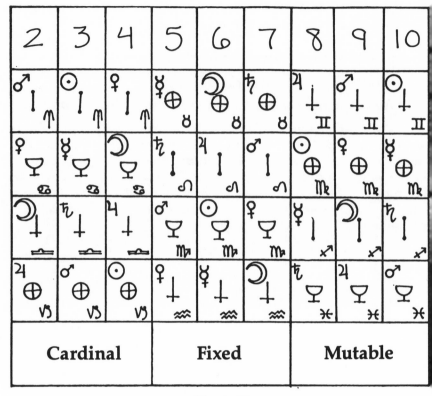

Figure 13
Cardinal, Fixed and Mutable Signs

The lines in the sign of Gemini, inscribed on the octahedron, are similar to those in the sign of Aries. Gemini has the addition of Jupiter in the west, and the deletion of Venus in the east. When including the three decanates of Gemini on the octahedron, we find the horizontal plane of the octahedron inscribed.

When inscribing the octahedron on the two dimensional glyph of the Tree of Life, it appears slightly distorted. When inscribed within the Cube, the dimensions are exact. This is seen when the four cardinal points of Jupiter, Mars, Venus, and Mercury are connected. This brings the four vulgar metals iron (Mars), copper (Venus), mercury (Mercury), and tin (Jupiter) into alignment with the Central Ego in Tiphareth, symbolic of gold and the Sun.

The other sign that forms the same triangle as Gemini on the octahedron is Capricorn through the influence of the 2, 3, 4 of Pentacles. The value of the letter Ayin attributed to Capricorn is 70. When reduced, 70= 7+0=7, it has the value of Zain, the letter attributed to Gemini. Key 15, The Devil, given to Capricorn, reduces to 15=1+5=6, the number of the Key of Gemini. Both Capricorn and Gemini are connected through the diagonal of Final Tzaddi. Through the path of Final Tzaddi the forces of Ayin are brought to bear on the currents of Gemini.

As one confronts the dweller on the threshold, Key 15, and pierces the veil of **Darkness,** thou shalt discover the **Angel of Redemption,** who will **Deliver** thee, with his **Right Hand,** from the **Oppression** of the illusion of separateness. Thou shalt climb **Jacob's Ladder,** to that place where thou shalt receive the **Law of the One,** who is **With Thee.** With **Thine Eye,** thou shalt find the **Seed of the Sun,** which is truly the **First Motion,** of the One Will, that rises in the east. With this seed thou shalt bloom into a **Pillar** in the house of God.

Creans Tenebras – "I create the darkness".

MLAK HGAL – Malewak Ha-Gawal – Angel of Redemption.

HTzLH – Hatazahlah – Deliverance.

IMINK – Yiminehkah – Thy right hand.

ONI – Aniy – Oppression.

SLM – Sullahm – The ladder of Jacob's dream.

SINI – Sinai – Where Moses received the Laws.

OMK – Immekah – With Thee.

OIN – Ayin – Eye.

Sperma Solis – Seed of the Sun, or Gold.

Primum Mobile – First Motion.

OMVDI – Ammudi – Pillars.[11]

These words, both the Hebrew and the Latin have a value of 130, the number of Ayin spelled in full (OIN), 70+10+50=130

The fourth sign in the Great Wheel is Cancer. Unlike the sign of Gemini, which is directly above and parallel Cancer and flows from south to north, the current of Cancer flows north to south. The current flows from the place of greatest darkness to greatest light.

The first decanate is ruled by Venus, the second decanate by Mercury, and the third by the Moon. The sign of Cancer completes the set of boundaries that bind the eastern face of the Cube. The east is the place of first light and the beginning of the cycles of creation.

Cancer receives the influence of Aries which flows from

above to the below. Aries is the time of the Vernal Equinox, and Cancer the time of the Summer Solstice. Astrologically, Cancer and Aries create a 90 degree aspect. In the northeastern below corner, the energies of the Equinox and the Solstice meet, and the creative intention established in the first decanate of Aries, which is ruled by Mars, has fructified the womb of Binah, the Bright Fertile Mother, and has brought forth manifestation, as is evidenced by the conditions at the end of spring and the beginning of summer. This point also joins together the forces of cardinal fire, and cardinal water, thus creating a hexagram of opposite cardinal, elemental forces.

On the octahedron, a triangle is formed connecting the above (Mercury), with the eastern (Venus), and below (Moon). The connection of the point of Venus, Mercury, and the Moon inscribe a triangle like those of Aries and Gemini with the exception of the plane on which this triangle is inscribed. The previous triangles of Aries and Gemini were inscribed on the horizontal plane. The triangle of Cancer connects points on the vertical plane, through the 2, 3, 4 of Cups. This is shown in the following diagram.

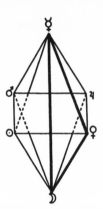

Figure 14
The placement of the 2, 3 and 4 of Cups

There is an interesting relationship between the above face and the eastern face of the Cube. They are the only two faces that have an energy flow that continue in the same direction and can be traveled indefinitely. The above face moves in a counterclockwise direction, and the eastern face moves in a clockwise direction. If they were considered as gears in a machine, they would continue to support each other in their movements, as gears within a clock move in harmony with each other, causing each to move in an opposite direction. When the center of each of these two faces are connected with the four corners that bind each face, a spiral vortex is generated, similar to a blender mixing liquid.

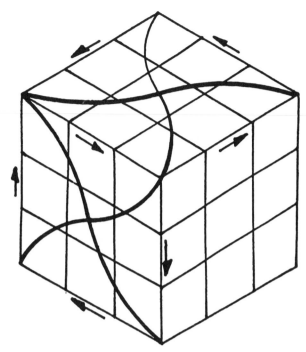

Figure 15
The Energy Flow of the Above and Eastern Faces

Cancer is the first of the below lines, and it has access to one of the diagonals. Final Kaph receives the influence of the east below line of Cancer/Cheth. It ascends from the southeast lower corner to the northwest above corner terminating at the point where Leo, Libra, and Sagittarius meet.

The combined energies of the four letters that bind the eastern face of the Cube have a value of 26, (Heh=5)+(Vav=6) +(Zain=7)+(Cheth=8)=26. This is the number of IHVH, and the number of the Cube when its boundaries (12), corners (8), and faces (6), are added together.

The sign that occupies the same line on the octahedron as Cancer is Aquarius through the 5, 6, 7 of Swords. The place where these two signs are united is through the ascending southeast corner of Taurus.

There is a profound development of lunar and venusian forces as the path of Cancer ascends the path of Taurus. The Moon is the ruling planet in the sign of Cancer. The Moon is the Prima Materia and is the universal substance which congeals into a specific form through a creative image. As the Prima Materia rises through the sign of Taurus, Venus, ruler of creative imagination, congeals this substance and brings the lunar force into specific manifestation, thus exalting the Moon in the sign of Taurus. "Its power is most perfect when it has again been changed into Earth".[12] Alchemically the sign of Cancer rules the operation of Separation.[13] What is separated is the infinite potential of Gimel into something kinetic. The sign of Taurus rules the alchemical operation of Congelation,[14] where that which is in a liquid state comes into an earthen form. The cardinal water of Cancer becomes fixed in the sign of Taurus.

Moving from the western to the eastern face via the south below line of Pisces/Qoph is the power of creative imagination in its exalted form. It is the revelation of the pure desire nature, which comes forth from the (ARIK ANPhIN), **The Vast Countenance,** the Crown of Primal Will. The sign of Pisces rules the alchemical operation of multiplication.[15] **The Corporeal Intelligence** communicates its desire nature to its centers of expression in their state of "separation".

There is a tremendous impact between the Prima Materia flowing through the sign of Cancer, and the exalted power of Venus through the path of Pisces. Both of these paths can be seen as tremendous rapids converging on a single point. The only possible outlet for this force is through the path of the **Triumphant and Eternal Intelligence** of the sign of Taurus, and the letter Vav. It is through this tremendous force that the exalted Venus in Pisces and the ruling Moon in Cancer bring forth the fixed Earth, where the Moon becomes exalted and Venus takes up rulership in the sign of Taurus.

The letter Gimel, associated with the Moon, spelt in full (GML), has a value of 73, the same value as Chockmah (ChKMH), which holds the infinite potential of the One. The word Chockmah speaks to the separating power of Cancer and the impact of the Corporeal Intelligence of Pisces when its letters are studied. The letter Cheth is representative of Cancer and the operation of separation. The letter Kaph, attributed to the planet Jupiter, is exalted in the sign of Cancer, and co-rules the sign of Pisces. The letter Mem is the higher octave of the Moon, which rules the sign of Cancer. Mem is also the Mother letter that forms the eastern face of the Cube, of which Cancer binds the below portion. The letter Mem is also the co-ruler of Pisces with Jupiter. The letter Heh, which is associated with the sphere of Saturn, is the sphere from which the letter Cheth and the sign of Cancer descend on the Tree of Life. Heh is also assigned to the cardinal sign of Aries, which descends on the northeast corner, from the above to the below face, where it joins the currents of Cancer.

The letter Gimel, also associated with the below face of the Cube, represents the subconscious mind and is the storehouse of memory, both personal and collective. Through the separating power of Cancer, the multiplication of Pisces, and the congealing power of Taurus, the infinite storehouse releases its substance so that it may be worked upon in the world of name and form by our self-conscious minds as it ascends to the upper face of the Cube.

When a specific idea or memory arrives in the above face, it is subject to dissolution through the power of Aquarius and the letter Tzaddi, the Natural Intelligence.

Through the power of meditation, which is the act of dissolution, the Divine Substance may be placed in **Order**, transforming the **Reprobate Earth** into the multiplied **Stone**, where the **Light of the World** will shine forth from **Mount Zion** and create a **New Mind**, that will receive the **Universal Science** from our **Mother Church**.

LOD – Lah-ad – Put in order

Terra Damnata – Reprobate earth

Lapis+ABN – Stone and stone – Latin and Hebrew

Lux Mundi – Light of the world

Mons Zion – Mount Zion, (signifies the brain)

NChMV – Nahemo – New mind

Ars Notaria – Universal science

Mater Ecclesia – Mother church[16]

These words all have a value of 104, which is the same value of the letter Tzaddi when it is spelt in full (TzDI).

It is through the power of Tzaddi that we are meditated upon and, therefore, meditate, and draw from the depths of the unconscious the great wisdom that lies there.

The next sign in the series is Leo. The first decanate is ruled by Saturn, the second is ruled by Jupiter and the third is ruled by Mars through the 5, 6, 7 of Wands. This creates a triangle connecting the northwest and the center point of the Cube as viewed in Figure 16.

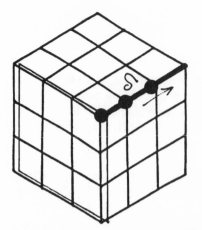
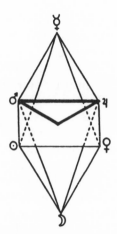

Figure 16
The placement of the 5, 6 and 7 of Wands

The sign of Pisces is the sign that occupies the same triangle as that of Leo, through the 8, 9, 10 of Cups. Final Kaph brings the full power of Pisces to bear on the full power of Leo. That is, Final Kaph begins at the completion of the south below line attributed to Pisces and terminates at the end of the north above line associated with Leo. Both signs have traversed the entire face of their placement before encountering Final Kaph. This brings the most sublime spirit of the Corporeal Intelligence, symbolic of Kether, to operate through the heart center, ruled by the Sun in Leo and symbolic of Tiphareth. Jupiter and Neptune co-rule the sign of Pisces. It is the power of the Stable Intelligence (Mem-Neptune) which is exalted in the sign of Leo. Jupiter also rules the second decanate in Leo and is the Intelligence Of **The Desirous Quest** (Kaph-Jupiter) which comes to full fruition in Final Kaph.

It is through the path of Final Kaph that we enter the **Interior of the Earth,** and open its metal, **Antimony,** and see **Thy Face** in **The Light of the Sun.** We then experience the peace of the **Stable Intelligence,** which allows us to see Thy **Beauty** through **Thine Eyes.**

Interiora Terrae – Interior of the earth.

ANTIMN – Antimony, metal of the earth.

PhNIK – Thy face.

Deus Lux Solis – God, light of the Sun.

QIIM – Qayam – Stable.

NOM – Noam – Beauty.

OINIK – Thine Eyes.[17]

The following words have a value of 160, which is the value of the intelligence of Mem/Neptune, which rules Pisces and is exalted in the sign of Leo.

The sign Virgo moves from the northeast below corner to the northwest below corner. It is ruled by the Sun in the first decanate, Venus in the second, and Mercury in the third decanate through the 8, 9, 10 of Cups. The points connected here are the southern, eastern and above faces of the Cube, as seen in Diagram 17.

 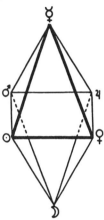

Figure 17
The placement of the 8, 9 and 10 of Pentacles

The zodiacal signs of Virgo and Libra do not have a partner occupying the same triangle as do the other signs.

They both terminate at the northwest below corner, where Final Tzaddi begins. Virgo brings forth the power of Mercury, for it is both ruler and exalted in this sign. The exalted spirit of Mercury in Virgo comes to rest through Final Tzaddi in mutable Gemini, where it takes dominion over mutable earth in Virgo and fixes the volatile substance in mutable air of Gemini. Mercury also merges with its higher octave, Uranus as the sign of Aquarius brings its influence to the southeast above corner, where Final Tzaddi terminates.

By traversing the path of Virgo and the letter Yod, **Man** may know the **Will** of the One, and be **Exalted** in the **Heavens**, through the power of the **Fiery Ones**.

ANSh – Enash – Man.

HRTzVN – Ha-Rahtzone – Will. (The intelligence of Will associated with Yod).

NShA – Nishshaw – Exalted.

ShMIA – Shemayah – Heavens.

AShIM – Ishim – The fiery ones. The choir of angels associated with Malkuth.[18]

These words all have a value of 351, the same value of Ha-Ratzone, the Will, the name of the intelligence of the letter Yod, and the sign of Virgo.

With one half of the year gone, we now move into the Autumnal Equinox and the sign of Libra. The first decanate is ruled by the Moon, the second by Saturn and the third ruled by Jupiter through the 2, 3, 4 of Cups. In the sign of Libra, the Chaldean order comes to a full completion in the planet Jupiter. The order begins again with the planet Mars where the patterns are repeated in the sign of Scorpio. It is from this point that the octahedron receives double coverage from the pairs of signs mentioned earlier.

In Libra, the points of the below, center, and western faces are connected.

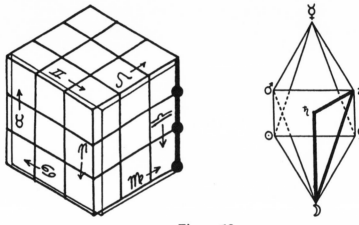

Figure 18
The placement of the 2, 3 and 4 of Swords

Libra like Virgo terminates at the northwest below corner where their influence may travel the diagonal of Final Tzaddi to the southeast above corner of the Cube. There is a profound circulation of subtle intelligences through Final Tzaddi and Final Kaph, which moves these intelligences from exaltation to rulership, and rulership to exaltation.

Libra begins in the northwest above corner, and descends to the northwest below corner. As Libra begins its descent, it receives the influence of Final Kaph, which brings the exalted power of Venus from Pisces to rulership in Libra. The ruling power of Nep-

une and Jupiter in the sign of Pisces impacts the sign of Leo (where
Neptune is exalted), and influences the sign of Sagittarius (where
Jupiter is ruler).

Now, Saturn is exalted in the sign of Libra. Through the de-
cent on the northwest corner, Libra brings the exalted influence of
aturn to rulership in the sign of Capricorn, whose current travels
rom the northwest below line to the southwest below line where it
icks up the sign of Pisces. This influence travels along the south be-
ow line of Pisces and returns to Libra through Final Kaph. This cir-
ulation of Saturn becomes purified after many cycles. The influence
f Saturn is finally transferred through Final Tzaddi and brought
nto rulership in the sign of Aquarius where the limiting power of
aturn is coupled with the expansive power of Uranus, which co-
ules Aquarius with Saturn. This influence then circulates on the
bove face of the Cube through the signs of Gemini, Leo, Sagittarius,
nd Aquarius, where it becomes integrated into self-consciousness.

> I Am the Knot in the endless cord of life,
> Binding Past to Future in the eternal Present.
> I am Aleph and Tav,
> Beginning and end.
> All that was,
> And all that shall be,
> Now is,
> For in mine eyes time is not.
> Therefore am I the outset of the quest,
> And also the goal thereof,
> And I am the Way of Life.[19]

When we look at the astrological influence of the letters asso-
iated with Libra, the creative process becomes well defined. Venus
ules the sign of Libra, and embodies the influence of the letter
Daleth. Saturn is exalted in Libra and receives the influence of the
etter Tav; the letter Lamed is attributed to Libra, and the combined
nfluence of these letters, D-Th-L, is the full spelling of Daleth, the
etter for Venus.

The letter Aleph descends into the sphere of Chockmah, and
ts influence arrives in the sphere of Binah through the path of
Daleth, Venus. Aleph, meaning Ox, is harnessed through the Ox-
oad, which is the meaning of Lamed, the letter of Libra. Through
he directive agency of Lamed, the creative powers of Daleth become
imited through the exaltation of Saturn, which brings a specific im-
ge into manifestation.

As the currents of Libra, located on the northwest corner, de-
cends into the western below line, we are confronted with the
Chaos of the cardinal Earth, in the sign of Capricorn, often called

the dweller on the threshold. This is the **Shadow of the Almighty.**
As we pass through this **Door,** into the sign of Pisces, we are then
able to drink the **Heavenly Dew,**[20] and experience the true **Essence
of Thy Father.**

BITh-HH-VV – Bohu (spelled in full) – Chaos

TzL ShDI – Tzale Shaddai – The Shadow of the Almighty

DLTh – Daleth(spelled in full) – Door

TL HShMIM – Tal Ha-shamahim – Dew of heaven.

ATh ABIK – Eth Abika – The essence of thy Father.[21]

The value of these words is 434, the same value as the astrological influence in the sign of Libra (DLTh)- Libra, Venus and Saturn

This completes the placement of the Minor Keys bearing the
numbers 2 through 10, which make up the 36 decanates of the zodia
cal wheel. The remaining Minor Keys, the Aces and Court Cards, an
placed within the boundaries of the twelve zodiacal lines.

Something of interest is encountered as one attempts to place
the Minor Arcana on the Cube of Space: the connecting of the point
which divided the cells of the Magic Square of Saturn was the resul
of trial and error. It can be observed that there are 56 such points on
the Cube. This immediately connected with the number of Keys in
the Minor Arcana, thirty-six Keys numbering from 2 through 10, 16
Court Cards, and 4 Aces, totaling 56. It would seem that there woul
be a spot for each Key, one for each point; this was found to be inac
curate. The only points where the Keys numbering 2 through 10 ma
be placed are on the 12 boundary lines associated with the 12 zodia
cial signs. The interior points formed by the Magic Square do not
contain lines attributed to the signs of the zodiac. This left 32 point
on the 12 boundary lines to place 36 Keys.

The observant reader will have seen by now that there are fou
points which are occupied by two Minor Tarot Keys. These points are
the northeast above corner, the southeast below corner, the northwes
below corner, and the southwest below corner.

Both the 2 of Wands and the 7 of Wands are ruled by the plan
et Mars and are located on the northeast above corner; the 2 of Wand
is located in Aries, while the 7 of Wands is located in Leo. The placement for these two Keys occurs at the same point. The 2 of Wands de
scends into the below face and the 7 of Wands circulates on the abov
face moving from east to west, along the north above line.

The 6 of Pentacles and the 4 of Cups are located on the south
east below corner. Both these decanates are ruled by the Moon; the
of Pentacles in the sign of Taurus, the 4 of Cups in Cancer. The 4 of

ups moves from the north to south, and the 6 of Pentacles moves
rom the below to the above.

The 2 of Pentacles and the 4 of Swords occupy the northwest
elow corner and are ruled by the planet Jupiter. This is the union of
ne forces of Jupiter in Libra through the 4 of Swords, and Jupiter in
apricorn through the 2 of Pentacles.

The final point containing two minor Keys is the below
outhwest corner. These are ruled by the planet Mars and are associ-
ted with the 5 and 10 of Cups. These are the signs of Scorpio with
he 5 of Cups, and Pisces with the 10 of Cups. The sign of Scorpio
rings the Mars influence to the above face, and Pisces brings the
Mars influence to the southeast corner, where it surfaces through the
ign of Taurus.

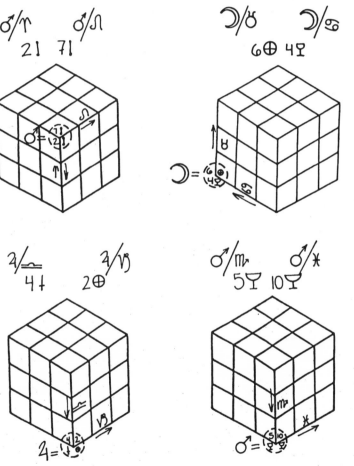

Figure 19
The Doubly-Ruled Corners on the Cube of Space

THE ACES

The next section to look at is the placement of the Aces. The Aces are associated with the sphere of Kether. It is the Aces that represent the descent of the intelligence of Kether, through the four worlds of Qabalah.

If we refer back to the octahedron, we will see that the sphere of Kether is placed on the above face of the Cube. It is on the above face that the 4 Aces are located. The Aces are placed on the 4 points, created by the Magic Square of Saturn that surround the central point of the upper face of the Cube. The following diagram shows the above face and the placement of the Aces.

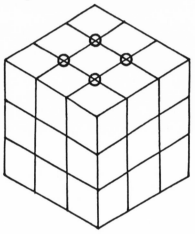

Figure 20
The placement of the Four Aces

Now, with the 36 decanates it is a rather simple process to determine the suit of each Key. Each Key carries the suit, or elemental quality, of the zodiacal sign that contains it. As far as the Aces are concerned, it is necessary to use a slightly different method, for the Aces rule different portions of the year and are not subject to the influence of one sign. The Aces actually rule the quarters of the year. Thus, each Ace influences three signs. The Ace of Wands rules the quarter of the year from the Vernal Equinox to the Summer Solstice, which includes the signs, Aries, Taurus, and Gemini. This covers the northeastern, southeastern, and eastern above lines.

The Ace of Cups rules the time of year from the Summer Solstice to the Autumnal Equinox, which includes the signs of Cancer, Leo, and Virgo. This touches the east below, north above, and the north below lines.

The Ace of Swords rules the time of year from the Autumnal quinox to the Winter Solstice, which includes the signs of Libra, orpio, and Sagittarius. This covers the northwest, southwest, and e west above lines.

The Ace of Pentacles rules the time of year from the Winter lstice to the Spring Equinox, which concludes the zodiacal year th Capricorn, Aquarius and Pisces. This covers the west below, uth above, and south below lines. The cycle repeats itself as one vels around the zodiacal wheel, or the Cube. The following is a agram showing the Aces and their position in the zodiacal year.

If we examine the model, 6 circles are tangent to a central 7th, Chapter 1, Figure 4. We can begin to see the symbolic quality of e Aces as they appear on

A. the upper face of the large Cube surrounding the central point, where Kether of the octahedron is placed;

B. how they fit in the uppermost vesica in the construction circles which join the negative veils of existence to the archetypal world;

C. how these four points descend through the cube defining a cubic column which defines the eight corners of the central Cube.

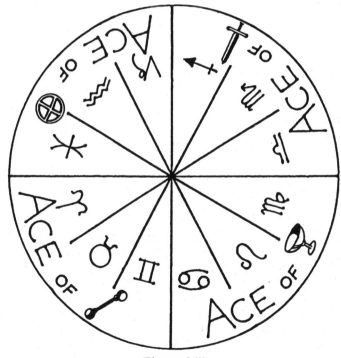

Figure 21[22]
The Four Aces and the quarters of the Year

These four vertical lines continually relate the Aces to Kether as being the first and the ONE; these points are also the 4 Kethers of the 4 Trees that exist on the 4 corners of the Cube, discussed in Chapter 3.

To relate suit quality to the 4 Aces can be accomplished by bisecting the vesica on which the Aces lie, from the northeast corner to the southwest corner. This line connects the zodiacal signs, Aries and Scorpio – one sign being fire and the other water. The Ace that rests at the end of the vesica near the northeast corner receives the suit of Wands. The Ace nearest the southwest corner receives the suit of Cups. If the same vesica is bisected from the southeast corner to the northwest corner, we would find that the Ace on the southeast corner is the Ace of Pentacles receiving the element of Earth from the sign of Taurus. The Ace on the northwest corner is the Ace of Swords receiving the quality of Air from the sign of Libra.

To summarize then, the Ace of Wands is closest to the northeast corner and the sign of Aries. The Ace of Cups is closest to the southwest corner and the sign of Scorpio. The Ace of Swords is closest to the northwest corner and the sign Libra. The Ace of Pentacles is closest to the southeast corner and the sign of Taurus.

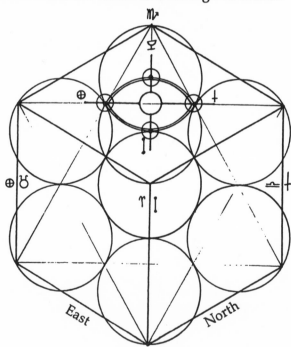

Figure 22
The suit attributions of the Aces

Since the 4 Aces surround the Kether of the octahedron and
e 4 Aces represent Kether in the 4 worlds of manifestation, the 4
es must have the same nature as the central idea, with a prepon-
rance in a particular element or world of the Qabalah. Notice that
the traditional two-dimensional glyph of the Tree of Life, the letter
eph is the first path to emanate from Kether. On the octahedron, it
Aleph that moves from the center to the above and from the center
the below. The Aces have the same quality as Kether for they are
ther and, hence, descend in parallel paths to the lower face.

This conclusion brings a couple of things to light: first, the 4
ints on the bottom of the Cube are directly beneath the 4 points of
e top of the Cube and represent the Aces as they make their trans-
rmation from one suit to another. This brings in a new under-
anding of the 4 final diagonals that pass through the central point
the Cube. The diagonals are the agents for bringing the influence
Kether from one world to another.

Second, it is the 4 diagonals that define the interior bound-
ies of the 27 cubic units. The 27th cube rests in the center of the
acrocosmic Cube. This occurs when the diagonals intersect the
rtical lines of the 4 Aces as the Aces descend from the above to the
low face of the Cube. The central cube is also the square root of
e Macrocosmic Cube.

As the 4 Aces descend, they form a cubic column. The center
this column is the axis of Aleph. The 4 vertical corners of this cu-
c column are bounded by the 4 Aces. The central Cube is the only
ube of the 27 cubic units that has none of its faces exposed to the
terior of the Cube. This central Cube and its boundaries further
clares that all manifestation is the result of a central act of inten-
on by the Central Self. This Central Self is omnipresent and ex-
nds its influence to all other points in space and chooses the limits
its self-expression. Every aspect of this central Cube speaks to the
Wonderful Intelligence" (ShKL PLA) of Kether. The following dia-
ram shows the Aces descending into the below face of the Cube.

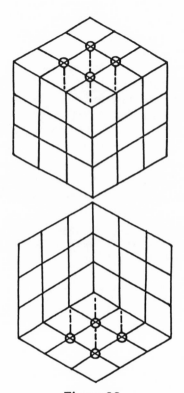

Figure 23
The Aces' movement from the Above to the Below

At this point, the Aces can be laid to rest and our attention directed to the 16 Court Cards, their placement on the Cube, their suit attribution, as well as their connection to different parts of the zodiacal year.

There is a sameness about the Kings, Queens and Knights, for they each rule three decanates, yet the decanates are not all in the same sign. The following diagram shows the Kings, Queens, and Knights as the appear in the zodiacal wheel.

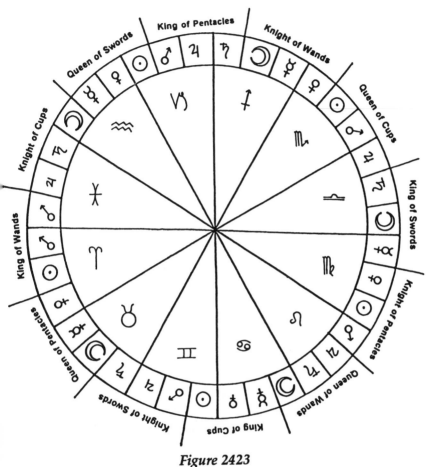

Figure 2423
The Court Cards and their placement in the Zodiacal year

The first Court Cards under consideration will be the Kings. The Kings are attributed to the sphere of Chockmah, the sphere of the Divine Father, and the Life Force, Chiah. In looking at Figure 24, we can see that the King of Wands rules the last decanate of Pisces and the first two decanates of Aries. The planet Mars, which represents the manifested Life Force, rules the last decanate of Pisces as well as the first decanate of Aries. So in these two signs, Pisces and Aries, we see a concentration of the Life Force, that is to awaken creation from sleep (Pisces rules the function of sleep, and the Medulla Oblongata which joins the spinal column to the brain). Pisces is also the transition point from the apparent slumber of winter to the awakening of spring; to utilizing the power of the higher centers of the brain, to organizing that which is coming forth from the creative mind of the All. In the sign of Pisces, the planet Venus, ruler of creative imagination, is exalted. Aries rules the brain and the function of reason, as well as ruling that which streams forth from the creative mind.

There remain at this time 16 points on the Cube where the Court Cards can be placed. This is great because there are only 16 cards left. The available spaces are in the cardinal points, north, south, east, and west. In the Tarot series, the planet Mars is attributed to the Life Force. Mars rules the brain center in the sign of Aries, as well as the center of power, expressed in sexual energy, in the sign of Scorpio. Mars is exalted in the sign of Capricorn where this force energizes and **Renews**[24] the mind for greater vision. The sphere on the Tree of Life attributed to this force is Geburah. This sphere or planetary influence has been placed on the northern face. Perhaps the most important point for the placement of the Court Cards is in the sealing of the 6 directions by IHV. When the above and below were sealed, it was with IHV, and IVH. The tip of the letter Yod is associated with Kether, and the above face. When IHV sealed the south and north, it was with VIH and VHI. Vav is the letter that descends from Chockmah, as does the letter Heh. Heh is located on the northeast corner and Vav on the southeast corner. The Holy Letter, Sheen, connects the center with the south and north. Sheen is the Mother of Fire, and manifests on the north through the planet Mars and in the south through the Sun. Since Mars rests in the north, so will the 4 Kings, which represent the 4 levels of condensation of the Life Force.

As the Aces surround the Kether of the octahedron, the Kings surround the sphere of Geburah on the northern face. These are not as obvious as the Aces; however, the same basic methods will be used to discover the suits of the Court Cards. The central vesica on the north face is used, as with the Aces, to determine the suit of each card. Using the same procedure, the vesica is bisected and the lines extended to the 4 corners of the northern face. The following diagram shows the extension of the bisecting lines and the signs from which the 4 Kings will receive their attributions.

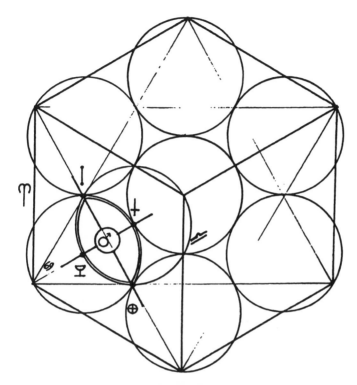

Figure 25
The placement and suit attributions of the Kings

The Kings are associated with the initiating quality of the
cardinal signs.[25] If we look at the northern face, we find that each
corner in some way is either receiving the influence of a cardinal
sign or flowing into a cardinal sign. On the northeast above corner,
Aries, the sign of cardinal fire, flows from the above to the below.
The point on the apex of the vesica closest to this corner is the King
of Wands. The corner directly below, which receives the influence of
cardinal fire, is cardinal water in the sign of Cancer. The point bisected on the vesica closest to this corner is the King of Cups. The
line which extends to the northwest above corner flows into the influence of cardinal air, in the sign of Libra, which descends into the
corner below. The point closest to this corner is the King of Swords.
The final point, the King of Pentacles, is nearest to the northwest below corner, which empties into the sign of cardinal earth, Capricorn.

The next set of Court Cards are the Queens. Their attributions will be defined using the same system. The Queens are associated with the Great Mother and the sphere of Binah. On the Tree of

Life, it is the path of Daleth which connects the sphere of Chockmah to the sphere of Binah which, in turn, transforms the sterile Saturn into the fruitful Mother. Binah is the beginning of manifestation, as is the direction east. The planet attributed to the eastern face of the Cube is Venus, and Key 3, The Empress, of the Tarot is connected with that sphere. Venus is also called the Great Mother. With all these associations, it seems appropriate that the Queens belong on the eastern face. In the sealing of the directions, the east was sealed with a HIV, and the west with a HVI. On the Tree of Life, Heh is associated with the sphere of Binah.

Like the Kings and the Aces, the Queens will be placed on the points surrounding the center of the eastern face. The vesica surrounding the center of the eastern face is bisected as with the Aces and Kings. As the Kings are attributed to the cardinal signs, so the Queens are given to the fixed signs,²⁶ which is in keeping with the idea that Binah is the fixing and limiting power. On the northeast above corner is the fixed sign of Leo. The point closest to this corner is the Queen of Wands. In the southeast above corner, the fixed sign of air, Aquarius, brings its influence to bear. The point closest to this corner is attributed to Swords. The line that extends to the southeast below corner takes the influence from the below to the above, and is attributed to the fixed earth of Taurus. The point closest to this corner is attributed to the Queen of Pentacles. Up to this point, things have been consistent. To continue in this vein, there is a need for the fixed sign of water; Scorpio exists on the other side of the Cube. It is accessible to the Queen of Cups through Final Nun. Nun is associated with the 50 gates of Binah, which the Queens represent. Other than the connection with the Final Nun, there is no fixed water on the eastern face. The following diagram shows the placement of the Queens.

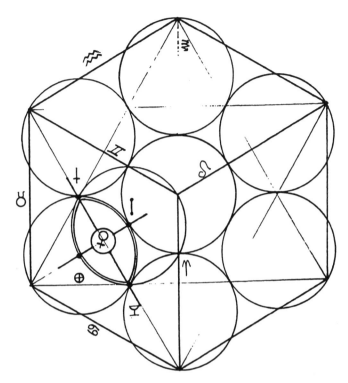

Figure 26
The placement and suit attributions of the Queens

The next group of Court Cards are the Knights. There are two
faces of the Cube left to chose from, the southern or western faces. A
reference to Ehben in Chapter 1 brings up the statement that the Father and Son are One. Now the Knights are placed in the sphere of
Tiphareth. Tiphareth is associated with the Son and the Sun, and receives the influence of Chockmah through the path of Heh, which is
attributed to Aries. Since Vav is associated with the Sun and Son,
and the Sun is on the southern face of the Cube, the Knights will be
placed here. As before, the same system of determining the suits will
be used. The vesica will be bisected with the Knights placed around
the sphere of the Sun. When bisecting the vesica, one line reaches the
southwest above corner, which receives the influence of mutable fire,
Sagittarius. The point closest to this sign is the Knight of Wands. The
line that extends to the southeast below face is carried by the influence of mutable water in the sign of Pisces. The point closest to
Pisces is the Knight of Cups. The line that extends to the southeast
above face flows into the current of mutable air and the sign of Gem-

ini. It is obvious at this time that the Knights are associated with the mutable signs. Once again, as with the Queens, one of the prescribed signs is missing; however, the mutable earth, which has escaped, is accessible through the final letter Peh descending through the sign of Aries and entering into the currents of Virgo. The following diagram shows the placement of the Knights.

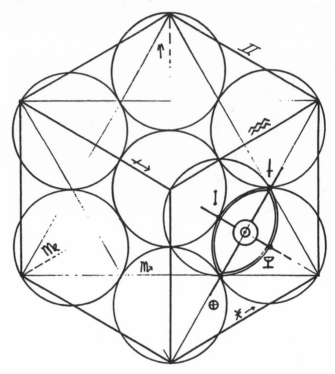

Figure 27
The placement and suit attributions of the Knights

The last of the Court Cards are the Pages. The only face left for their placement is the west. It is not merely by process of elimination that the Pages are placed in the west. As the Father and Son are one, so are the Mother and Daughter. A couple of other points indicate this: the Queens are associated with the sphere of Binah; the Pages with the sphere of Malkuth. Malkuth is defined through the power of Saturn. This is seen by looking at the Magic Square of Saturn, which defines the Cube of Space, symbol of the Earth, the sphere of Binah which derives the Magic Square of Saturn and the final path descending on the Tree of Life, the 32nd path, associated with the letter Tav which is also associated with Saturn.

The sphere of Malkuth is the vessel in which these Saturnine influences are poured. The Queens in the east represent the beginning of things, and the Pages in the west represent the completion of those things begun in the east. Furthermore, the sphere of Malkuth is also called the Bride who becomes the Mother for the next series of manifestation.

The same process as before will be used in finding the suit of the Pages. The Pages differ from the other Court Cards in the realm of association with the three decanates, for the Pages rule the quarters of the year, as do the Aces. Kether is in Malkuth, and Malkuth in Kether. When the bisecting line is drawn to the northwest above corner, the influence of the fixed fire of Leo is picked up. The line extended to the southwest below corner hits the sign of cardinal water in Cancer. The line that extends to the southwest above corner picks up the influence of fixed water in the sign of Scorpio. The line extending to the northwest below line picks up the influence of cardinal air in the sign of Libra. In this particular set of Court Cards, there is a sampling of two cardinal and two fixed signs.

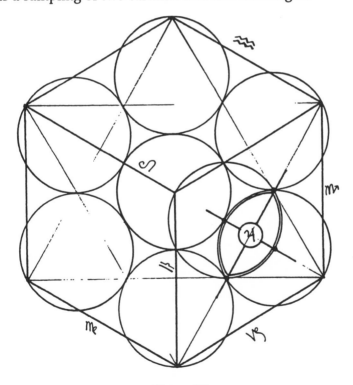

Figure 28
The placement and suit attributions of the Pages

As far as ruling the different quarters of the year are concerned, the Pages rule suit by suit and sign by sign as the Aces. The following chart shows the Pages in their ruling quarters.

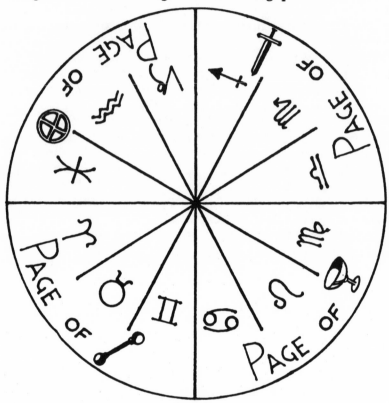

Figure 29
The Pages and the quarters of the Year

This completes the chapter on placement of the Minor Arcana. The next step is to discover how the Minor Arcana becomes the binding forces for the 27 cubic units that make up the Macrocosmic Cube of Space.

FOOTNOTES

The Tarot by Dr. Paul Foster Case.

Ibid

Idea taken from *The Power of Aleph-Beth,* by Philip S. Berg.

The Tarot of The Bohemians, by Papus.

SC, by Dr. Paul Foster Case.

The Sepher Yetzirah, Chapter 1:11

The Qabalistic Tarot, by Robert Wang.

Les Philosophers de Nature, First Year Spagyrics.

EA, and *OT,* by Dr. Ann Davies and Dr. Paul Foster Case.

Ideas taken from *TL, GW,* by Dr. Paul Foster Case.

Gematria collected from *ML,* by Dr. Paul Foster Case.

Tabula Smaragdina Hermetis, Secret Symbols of the Rosicrucians. Amorc edition.

GW;40:1, by Dr. Paul Foster Case.

GW;38:1, by Dr. Paul Foster Case.

GW;48:1, by Dr. Paul Foster Case.

Gematria collected from *The Magical Language,* by Dr. Paul Foster Case.

Ibid

Gematria collected from *The Magical Language* by Paul Foster Case.

Meditation of Qoph, from *The Book of Tokens,* by Paul Foster Case.

According to several alchemical texts, the Dew that condenses while the Sun is in the sign of Taurus contains a greater amount of Nitre, the universal spirit. This is to be collected and consumed, or used to enhance medicines. In some Rosicrucian texts from the 17th century, they speak of the actual generation of gold from this **Heavenly Dew.**

Gematria collected from *The Magical Language,* by Paul Foster Case.

Tarot of the Bohemians, by Papus.

Tarot of the Bohemians by Papus.

The Renewing Intelligence is the intelligence attributed to the sign of Capricorn and the letter Ayin.

OT;18:1, by Dr. Paul Foster Case.

Ibid

CHAPTER FIVE

THE 27 CUBIC UNITS

he reader may find this chapter difficult at first because of the language used to describe the boundaries of the 27 cubic units. For the sake of clarity, each description will be followed by a diagram to highlight the areas discussed. This chapter is presented to the reader in order to show the placement of each of the Minor Keys, and their astrological influences, as they appear on each of the 27 cubic units of the Macrocosmic Cube of Space.

THE BOUNDARIES OF THE 27 CUBIC UNITS

As with the Macrocosmic Cube, the 27 Microcosmic Cubes have their own defining lines. As the limiting power of Saturn becomes more condensed, the forms become more individualized. On the boundaries of the microcosmic cubes, there is a more complex union of the forces of the twenty- two Chaldean letters. As we look at the diagram of the Magic Square of Saturn, the 27 cubic units become visible. The Keys of the Minor Arcana, are located on the points that define the 27 cubes, as shown in Figure 5 of Chapter 4. There are four different types of situations concerning the 27 cubes. First, the cubes on the eight corners have 3 faces, 7 corners, and 9 boundary lines exposed to the outer surface of the larger cube. These eight corner cubes are bounded by 2 Court cards, 4 Minor Keys, and 1 Ace.

Figure 1

Second, the cubes located between the corners have 2 faces, 6 corners, and 7 boundary lines exposed. These lines are bounded by 2 Aces, 2 Court Cards, and 2 Minor Keys.

Figure 2

Third, the cubes in the center of each face have 1 face, 4 corners and 4 boundary lines exposed. They are bounded by 4 Court Cards on the cardinal faces and two Aces on the above and below interior faces.

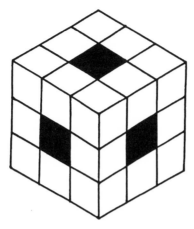

Figure 3

Fourth the 27th cubic unit is unseen from the outside. It is
surrounded by the other 26 cubes, and it has no faces, corners, or
boundary lines exposed to the exterior of the Cube, and is surrounded by the four Aces on all corners.

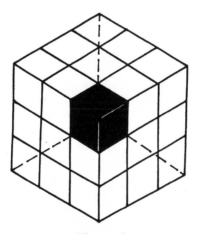

Figure 4

Each face of a cubic unit will receive the same directional
flow of energy as the face of the Macrocosmic Cube on which it
rests. For example, the above face of the above center cubic unit will
move in the same counter- clockwise direction, as the above face of
the Macrocosmic Cube. Cubic units on the eastern face have an energy flow in the clockwise direction, as does the eastern face of the
Macrocosmic Cube.

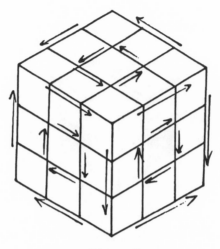

Figure 5

At this point, we must use the limiting power of Saturn and pick one of the 27 cubes, and begin this work. Since the six directions of the Cube of Space were sealed from the center, the central cubic unit seems like a logical place to start.

The process of sealing the six directions by (IHV), through the three Mother letters takes on a different form when we address the 27 cubic units. The central cube holds the initial intention, and sends forth this intention through the agency of the three Mother Letters. This time instead of the lines that extend from the center (as seen in Figure 6 of Chapter 1), we have a cubic column that extends from the same central point. The direction of a cubic column indicates which Mother letter is being expressed.

The Cubic Column of Aleph

On the line of Aleph, there is a cubic column which extends from the center to the above, and from the center to the below (see Figure 23 of Chapter 4). This cubic column is bounded on all sides by the four Aces. If we bring our attention to the vertical lines that descend from the four above corners of the central cubic unit on the above face, we will see that they connect with the central cube of the below face. If these vertical lines were divided in segments equaling the length of the boundary lines of the small cubes, they would intersect the four final diagonals, which would form the eight corners that define the 27th Central Cube.

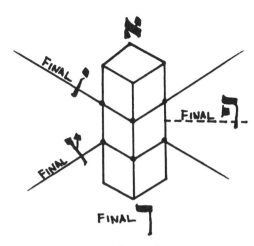

Figure 6
The Inscription of the Central Cubic Unit

This central cube is not only bounded by four Aces. It is also bounded by the points of intersection on the four diagonals. These points on the four diagonals receive the Mezlah, of the four Aces and the Central Cube, and bring this influence to the exterior faces of the Cube. This cubic column is similar to the column shown descending the Tree of Life in Figure 4 of Chapter 3. Once again, the four diagonals begin to take on a different meaning as channels. They do more than simply connect diametrically opposed corners.

Since the diagonals ascend from the below corners to the above diametrically opposite corners, we can see the profound relationship between the sub, Super, and self-conscious states.

In Key 6, **THE LOVERS**, the man (self-consciousness), looks to the woman (subconsciousness). The woman, however, looks to the Archangel Raphael, where she receives the superconscious impulse, and reflects it to self-consciousness, through the agency of subconsciousness.[1]

This same relationship exists on the below face of the Cube.

Subconsciousness brings the influence of the Central Cube (superconsciousness) to the above face (self-consciousness) through the agency of the four diagonals.

The above and below cubes of this cubic column are also bounded by Aces on all corners. The above face of the below cube is the below face of the Central Cube. The above face of the central cube, is the below face of the uppermost cube of this cubic column

(See Figure 4, Chapter 3). It is the Central Cube that radiates the intelligence outward to all other cubes; for all other cubes have access to the central cube, just as Tiphareth on the Tree of Life has access to all other Sephiroth on the Tree.

The central cubic column is a cubic form of the above to below axis of Aleph, Key 0, **The Fool.**

THE CUBIC COLUMN OF MEM

Following the outward flow of energy of the Central Cube from the center to the east and the west, we find the horizontal cubic axis of the Mother letter of Mem, The **Hanged Man.** As with the axis of Aleph, the center of this axis has its origin in the central cubic unit. On the eastern face, the axis of Mem is bounded by the four Queens on the outside, and the Aces of Wands and Pentacles on the interior western face. These are the eight corners of the eastern cube on the axis of Mem.

Notice that there is a transfer of the powers of Kether (the Aces) to Binah (the Queens). The eastern portion of the axis of Mem is similar to the 12th path on the Tree of Life, where the intelligence of Kether energizes the sphere of Binah.

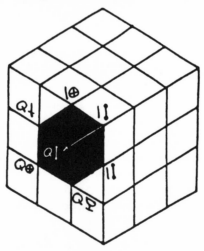

Figure 7

THE EASTERN CUBIC UNIT OF MEM

The western cubic unit on the axis of Mem is bounded by the four Pages on the outside, and the Aces of Cups and Swords on the interior face.

As with the eastern face of the cube, we see a transfer of the powers of Kether to the sphere of Malkuth, symbolized by the Pages. There is no direct link between the sphere of Kether and the sphere of Malkuth on the Tree of Life; however, both the Pages and the Aces govern the identical portions of the zodiacal year. This reminds us that Kether is in Malkuth and Malkuth is in Kether, but in a different manner.

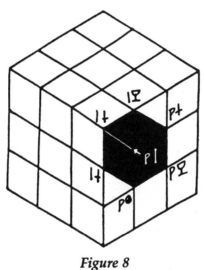

Figure 8

THE WESTERN CUBIC UNIT OF MEM

With the definition of the central, eastern and western cubic units, we now have a cubic cross which is made up of the cubic axes of Aleph and Mem, as seen in Figure 9.

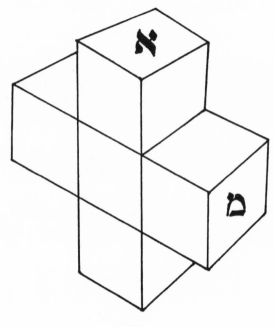

Figure 9
The Cubic Cross

This cross receives a second horizontal axis when the axis of Sheen is considered.

THE CUBIC COLUMN OF SHEEN

The northern cube on the axis of Sheen, is bounded by the four Kings on the exterior, the Aces of Wands and Swords on the southern interior face.

It is on this axis that we can see the transfer of intelligence from the sphere of Kether, to the sphere of Chockmah, symbolized by the Kings. The 11th path of Aleph which descends from Kether energizes the sphere of Chockmah.

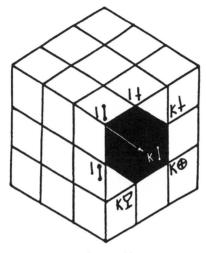

Figure 10

The central cube of the southern face is bounded by the four
_nights on the exterior, and the Aces of Cups and Pentacles on the
_terior northern face.

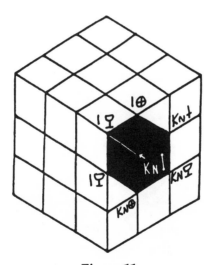

Figure 11

These three cubic columns bring the three Mother letters into
different expression, from a two dimensional to a three dimension-
l cubic, double-armed cross, as seen in Figure 12.

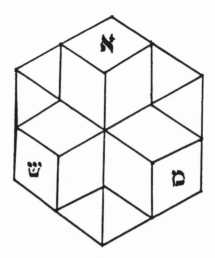

Figure 12
The Double-Armed Cubic Cross

This completes the description of the 7 cubic units which seal the six directions from a central seventh cube, forming the Gnostic Cross in a cubic form.

The next units to focus on, are the cubes that fill in the double-armed cross to create three squares on three different planes, as seen in Figure 13.

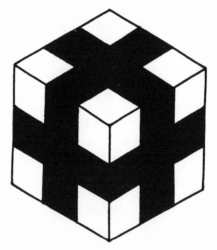

Figure 13

THE CUBIC SQUARE OF ALEPH-MEM

We have seen the central cubic column, which is inscribed on all corners by the 4 Aces, which completely surround the above and below axes of Aleph. If we consider the axis of Mem and its central cubic units to the east and west, we can see a vertical cubic column extending to the above and below from these east/west units. These cubic columns are parallel with the central axis of Aleph.

Figure 14

The horizontal cubic column of Mem is at a 90 degree angle to the vertical axis of Aleph. The cubic units above and below the eastern and western central cubes take on the qualities of the axes of Aleph and Mem. They represent the union of these forces as a self-conscious and subconscious expression.

The eastern face of the Macrocosmic Cube is representative of beginnings. Through the combined forces of Aleph and Mem we have a value of 41 (AM), whose meaning is Womb, Origin, and Mother, and (GBVL) Gabal, meaning Boundaries. It is the eastern face that expresses the first quarter of the zodiacal year, in the signs of Aries, Taurus, Gemini. (ALI) My God, as well as (Amor) Love, in the Latin, have a value of 41, the value of Aleph-Mem.

On the above cube of the eastern central cubic column, we find the cube bounded on the above western corners by the Aces of Pentacles and Wands. The eastern above corners are bounded by the 9 of Swords to the south and the 8 of Swords to the north. The eastern below corners are bounded by the Queen of Wands to the north and the Queen of Swords to the south. The western below corners are bounded by the same Aces as the above western face, for the Aces descend from the above to the below. The combined keys are:

Ace of Pentacles	Ace of Wands
9 of Swords	8 of Swords
Queen of Wands	Queen of Swords

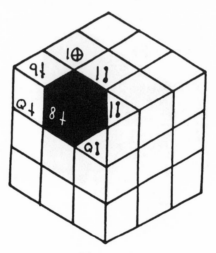

Figure 15

The below cube of this column is bounded by the Queen of Pentacles to the southeast above, the Queen of Cups to the northeast above. The southeast below is bounded by the 3 of Cups, and the northeast below by the 2 of Cups. The interior corners are bounded by the Aces of Pentacles to the southwest and Wands to the northwest.

Ace of Pentacles   Ace of Wands
Queen of Pentacles   Queen of Cups
3 of Cups   2 of Cups

Figure 16

This completes the central vertical eastern cubic column. There are now two vertical columns stacked side by side; these are the cubic column of Aleph and the central cubic column of Aleph-Mem. The above and below eastern cubes of the central cubic column fill in the spaces of the cubic cross in the east and have begun to create a cubic square that will be completed when the western central cubic column is defined.

On the western face, we have a similar situation as in the east. Both the energies of Aleph and Mem are expressed. The western face however represents the completion of things begun in the east.

When that which has begun in the east is completed in the west, there is an addition or multiplication of the conditions which took place in the east as they manifest in the west. The multiplication is similar to a single seed of corn which yields a hundred new seeds when it comes to fruition.

If we were to take the number 41, which is the value of Aleph-Mem, and add the letter Vav, which joins things together as the conjunction **"and,"** we have the value of 47. This is the value of (BID-AL) Be-Yad-EL, by the hand of God, and in the Latin, vita, life. The letter Kaph, which is the letter assigned to the west, means the hand in the act of grasping. The west shows the handiwork of the One.

The western above central cube is bounded on the east above corners by the Ace of Swords to the north and Ace of Cups to the south. These Aces bind the below north and south corners as well. On the western above corners, the 9 of Wands binds the north and the 10 of Wands holds the south. On the below western face of this cube, we have the Page of Wands to the north and Page of Swords to the south.

Ace of Swords	Ace of Cups
9 of Wands	10 of Wands
Page of Wands	Page of Swords

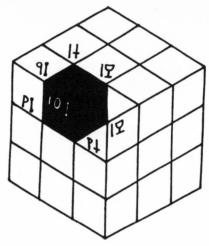

Figure 17

Next the below cube of the central western cubic column is
fined. It is bounded on the northwestern above corner by the Page
Pentacles. The outhwestern above corner is bounded by the Page
Cups. The northwestern below corner is held by the 3 of Penta-
:s. The southwestern below corner is bounded by the 4 of Penta-
:s. The northwestern above and belowcorners are bounded by the
:e of Swords. The above and below southwestern corners are
·unded by the Ace of Cups.

Ace of Cups	Ace of Swords
Page of Pentacles	Page of Cups
3 of Pentacles	4 of Pentacles

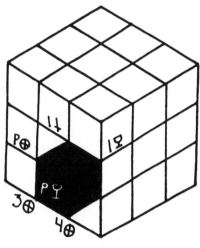

Figure 18

The first of three cubic squares is now formed. This cubic square forms a solid wall which divides the Macrocosmic Cube in the center from the central cubic column in the east, through the central cubic column in the center to the central Western cubic column, as seen in Figure 19.

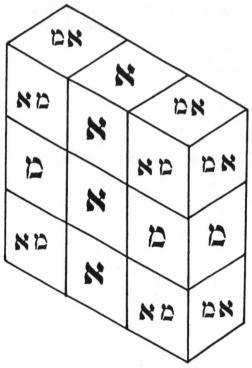

Figure 19
The Cubic Square of Aleph-Mem

The next cubic square is formed by filling in the arms of the cubic cross formed through the axis of the Mother letter Sheen. As the axis of Mem formed a relationship between itself and Aleph, we find the letter Sheen doing the same.

The combined value of Aleph and Sheen is 301, The Faithful King, and (ISh), meaning fire, foundation. This word is also used as a description for the entity of man. These two words have a value of 301, and give an idea of the energy of the union of the influences of Sheen and Aleph.

We begin in the northern portion of the axis of Sheen and bring our attention to the central cubic column in the north. The above cube of this cubic column is bounded in the southwest above corner by the Ace of Swords. The southeast above corner is bounded by the Ace of Wands. These Aces descend and form the southwest and the southeast below corner. The northwest above corner is bounded by the 5 of Wands and the northeast above corner by the 6 of Wands. The northwest below corner is bounded by the King of Swords, while the northeast below corner is bounded by the King of Wands.

Ace of Wands	Ace of Swords
5 of Wands	6 of Wands
King of Swords	King of Wands

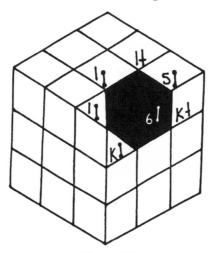

Figure 20

The below cube of this central northern cubic column is bounded by the King of Cups in the northeast above corner and the King of Pentacles in the northwest above corner. The northeast below corner is bounded by the 9 of Pentacles and the northwest below is bounded by the 8 of Pentacles. The above and below interior eastern corners are bounded by the Ace of Wands, and the above and below interior western corners are bounded by the Ace of Swords.

Ace of Wands	Ace of Swords
King of Cups	King of Pentacles
9 of Pentacles	8 of Pentacles

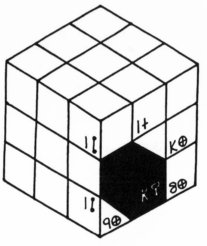

Figure 21

This fills in the northern portion of the cubic cross. We now have a cubic column formed in the north which is parallel with the central axis of Aleph.

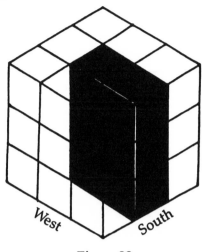

Figure 22

We now move to the southern face as we bring our attention to its central cubic column. The above cube is bounded in the northwest above corner by the Ace of Cups. The northeast above corner is bounded by the Ace of Pentacles. The southwest above corner is bounded by the 6 of Swords, and the southeast above corner is bounded by the 7 of Swords. On the below portion of the Cube, we find the southwest corner bounded by the Knight of Wands. The southeast below corner is bounded by the Knight of Swords.

As with the inner boundaries of all cubic units, both above and below have Aces as the binding force.

Ace of Cups	Ace of Pentacles
6 of Swords	7 of Swords
Knight of Wands	Knight of Swords

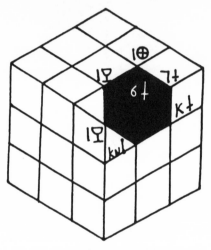

Figure 23

The below cubic unit of the central southern cubic column is bounded in the northwestern above corner by the Ace of Cups. On the above northeastern corner, the Ace of Pentacles is found. The above southwestern corner is bounded by the Knight of Pentacles. The above southeastern corner is bounded by the Knight of Cups. The southwestern below corner is bounded by the 9 of Cups. The below southeastern face is bounded by the 8 of Cups.

Ace of Cups	Ace of Pentacles
Knight of Pentacles	Knight of Cups
8 of Cups	9 of Cups

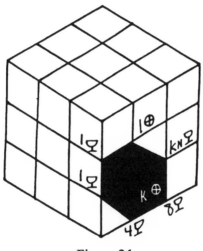

Figure 24

This completes the second cubic square of Aleph-Sheen, on the Macrocosmic Cube.

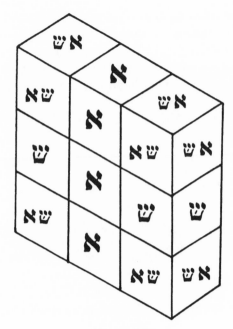

Figure 25
The Cubic Square of Aleph-Sheen

Figure 26 shows the square of Aleph-Sheen in relationship to the first cubic square formed from the axes of Aleph-Mem. Notice that the two cubic squares intersect and share the above and below central cubic axis of Aleph which is completely bounded by the 4 Aces.

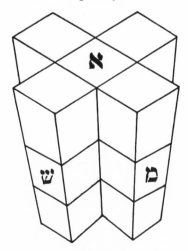

Figure 26
The Horizontal Cross within the Cube

There is one cubic square left to define. This is the horizontal cubic square created through the relationship between Mem and Sheen.

The value of the combined influences of Mem and Sheen is 340. Now the formation of the Mem and Sheen axes is a direct result of the sealing of the above and below faces of the cube by the Divine Being IHV, through the agency of Aleph. The remaining two axes of Mem and Sheen are a sprouting forth from the first root of Aleph. Netzer (NTzR), whose value is 340, means to sprout or the shoot of a branch. Shem (ShM), whose value is 340, is the actual combination of Mem-Sheen. It means a name or a form set apart from the whole. In the Qabalah, there are 72 variations of the Holy Name (Shem)-Hamphorash, which are equally divided throughout the boundaries of the Cube of Space. They reside within the 72 quinances, which divide the 36 decanates in half, thus creating 72 forms for This Holy Name.

All of the cubic units in this cubic square are located in the center of each face and corner of the Macrocosmic Cube. Note that in this relationship between Mem and Sheen, the cubic square is formed on a horizontal plane, instead of the vertical plane as in the case with Aleph-Mem, and Aleph-Sheen.

Figure 27

The first of these cubic units will be the northeast central cubic unit. This unit is bounded on the southwest above and below corners by the Ace of Wands. The northeast above corner is bounded by the 3 of Wands. The northwest above corner is bounded by the

King of Wands. The southeast above corner is bounded by the
Queen of Wands. On the northeast below corner the 4 of Wands is
the binding influence. The northwest below corner is bounded by
the King of Cups. The southeast below corner is bounded by the
Queen of Cups.

Ace of Wands	3 of Wands
4 of Wands	King of Wands
King of Cups	Queen of Wands
Queen of Cups	

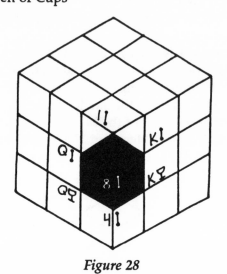

Figure 28

Since the central cubic units on each cardinal face of the
Macrocosmic Cube have already been defined through the agency of
Aleph-Mem (east and west center), and Aleph-Sheen (north, south
center), we need only deal with the central units on each corner. The
next unit, therefore, will be the northwest center cube.

On the above corners of this cube, we find the southeast bounded by the Ace of Swords, the southwest bounded by the Page of Wands. The northwest is bounded by the 2 of Swords. The northeast corner is bounded by the King of Swords. On the below corners, we find the northeast bounded by the King of Pentacles, the northwest bounded by the 3 of Swords, the southwest bounded by the Page of Pentacles.

Ace of Swords	King of Swords
King of Pentacles	Page of Wands
Page of Pentacles	2 of Swords
3 of Swords	

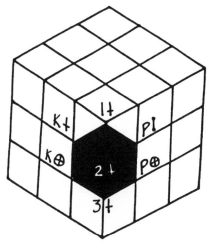

Figure 29

In the southwest corner, the central cube is bounded on the northeast above and below corner by the Ace of Cups. The above southeast corner is bounded by the Knight of Wands. The southeast below corner is bounded by the Knight of Pentacles. The southwest above corner is bounded by the 7 of Cups, the southwest below corner is bounded by the 6 of Cups. The northwest above corner is bounded by the Page of Swords, while the northwest below corner is bounded by the Page of Cups.

The Ace Cups	The Knight of Wands
The Knight of Pentacles	The 7 of Cups
The 6 of Cups	The Page of Swords
The Page of Cups	

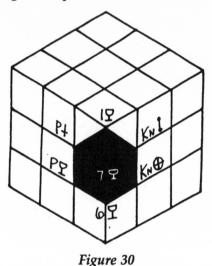

Figure 30

The final cubic unit of this horizontal cubic square lies on the center of the southeast corner. This cubic unit is bounded by the Ace Pentacles on the northeast above and below corners. The Knight Swords binds the southwest above corner, as the Knight of Cups nds the southwest below corner. The southeast abov is bounded the 5 of Pentacles, and the southeast below is bounded by the 7 of ntacles. The Queen of Swords binds the northeast above corner as e Queen of Pentacles holds the corner of the northeast below. This mpletes the horizontal cubic square under the influence of Mem-een.

Ace of Pentacles	Knight of Cups
Knight of Swords	Queen of Swords
Queen of Pentacles	5 of Pentacles
7 of Pentacles	

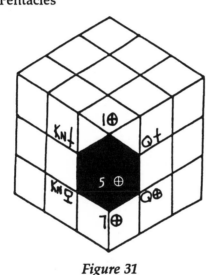

Figure 31

THE EIGHT CORNERS

With the three cubic squares defined through the agency of the Minor Arcana we have a visual effect similar to a Christmas package with 3 ribbons wrapped around it. Notice that there are 8 cubic units that have not been expressed within the three cubic squares. These are the 8 corners of the Macrocosmic Cube.

Figure 32
The Three Squares of Aleph, Mem and Sheen

There is something of great interest regarding these corners. If the reader would refer to Figure 13 of Chapter 3 you will see that the above corners are attributed to the invisible sphere of Daath, the sphere of Knowledge, and the below corners are attributed to the sphere of Malkuth, the sphere attributed to the earth and the fruit of the Tree of Life. In a sense, neither of these spheres are seen as part of the Tree of Life, rather as separated spheres, one fallen (Daath), the other landed in the world of form (Malkuth). These corners, above and below are not visibly part of the Aleph-Mem, Aleph-Sheen, and Mem-Sheen cubic squares.

These corners of Daath and Malkuth are connected to the central cubic unit through the medium of the four final diagonals, with the fifth final letter (Mem) located in the center. The five final letters thus bring forth 27 letters of the Aleph-Beth, one for each cubic unit in the Macrocosmic Cube. These final letters ripen the (Daath), knowledge into the world of (Malkuth), the Kingdom. In spite of the appearance of the separateness of Daath and Malkuth, they are forever connected to each other and the central cubic unit by the means of the final letters.

Beginning in the northeast above corner, we find a cube with fiery quality. It receives the influence of Gemini from the south, initiates the influence of Leo in the west, and Aries flowing to the below face. The Minor Keys that bind this cube are, The Ace of Wands on the southwest above and below corner. On the northwest above corner, we have the 6 of Wands, Jupiter/Leo, holding the corner. On the northwest below corner the King of Wands creates the boundary. The northeast above corner is doubly ruled with the 2 of Wands, Mars/Aries, and the 7 of Wands, Mars/Leo. The northeast below corner is the 3 of Wands Sun/Aries. Moving to the eastern portion of this cube, we have the southeast above corner bounded by the 10 of Swords, Sun/Gemini, and the southeast below bounded by the Queen of Wands, which rules the last decanate in Cancer and the first two decanates in Leo.

The Ace of Wands	The 2 of Wands
The 3 of Wands	The 6 of Wands
The 7 of wands	The Queen of Wands
The King of Wands	The 10 of Swords

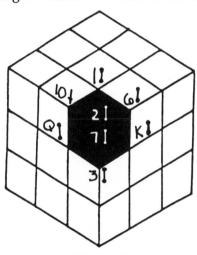

Figure 33

In relationship to this particular cube, we find that it is represented by the first and second decanates of the zodiacal year, by the 1-3 of Wands in which both the Ace and King of Wands rule. Since the northeast above corner is ruled both by Mars in Aries, and Mars in Leo, we find this same corner being influenced by the 2 and 7 of

Wands. With the exception of the 10 of Swords, Sun/Gemini, the entire cube is ruled by the element of fire, as seen by the presence of eight of the fourteen Minor Keys from that suit.

The northeast below cube is bounded on the southwest above and southwest below corners by the Ace of Wands. The northeast above corner is bounded by the 4 of Wands. The northeast below corner is held by the 10 of Pentacles. The southeast above corner is bounded by the Queen of Cups, while the southeast below corner is bounded by the 2 of Cups. The northwest above corner is bounded by the King of Cups and the northwest below corner is bounded by the 9 of Pentacles.

Ace of Wands	Queen of Cups
King of Cups	4 of Wands
2 of Cups	10 of Pentacles
9 of Pentacles	

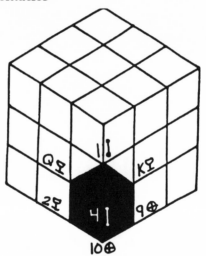

Figure 34

This particular corner has a blend of three Wands, three Cups and two Pentacles. This cube receives its influence from the fiery sign of Aries as it descends from the above to the below. At the bottom corner, the energy is divided where the currents flow either into the sign of Cancer or the sign of Virgo.

Moving to the northwest above corner of the Macrocosmic Cube, we find the cubic unit residing there bounded on the south-west above and below corners by the Ace of Swords. The northeast above corner is bounded by the 5 of Wands. The northeast below corner is held by the King of Swords. The northwest above corner is bounded by the 8 of Wands, while the northwest below corner is bounded by the 2 of Swords. The southwest above corner is bound-ed by the 9 of Wands, and the southwest below corner is bounded by the Page of Wands.

Ace of Swords	King of Swords
Page of Wands	5 of Wands
8 of Wands	2 of Swords
9 of Wands	

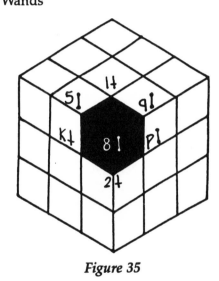

Figure 35

This particular cube shows the influence of both fire and air, the presence of the four keys from the suit of Swords/air and the four keys from the Wands/fire suit. The fiery sign of Leo moves from east to west, and terminates in this cube, and moves into both the mutable fire of Sagittarius, and the cardinal air of Libra.

Next we see the northwest below cubic unit bounded on the southeast above and below corner by the Ace of Swords. The northeast above corner is bounded by the King of Pentacles while the northeast below corner is bounded by the 8 of Pentacles. The northwest above corner is bounded by the 3 of Swords, and the northwest below corner is doubly ruled by the 4 of Swords and the 2 of Pentacles. The southwest above corner is bounded by the Page of Pentacles and the southwest below corner is held by the 3 of Pentacles.

Ace of Swords	King of Pentacles
Page of Pentacles	8 of Pentacles
3 of Swords	4 of Swords
3 of Pentacles	2 of Pentacles

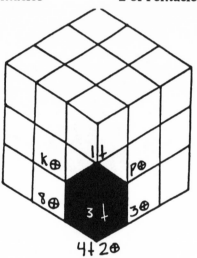

Figure 36

As the above cube on this northwest corner showed the influence of fire and air, this below corner shows the influence of air and earth. It is here that the influence of the cardinal air Libra, and the mutable earth of Virgo come together and are forced to merge with the cardinal earth of Capricorn, symbol of the dweller at the threshold.

The cubic unit on the southwest above corner is bounded on
he northeast above and below corners by the Ace of Cups. The
northwest above corner is bounded by the 10 of Wands, while the be-
ow corner of the northwest is held by the Page of Swords. The
southwest above corner is bounded by the 5 of Swords, and the
southwest below corner is bounded by the 7 of Cups. The southeast
above corner is held by the 6 of Swords, and the southeast below
corner is bounded by the Knight of Swords.

Ace of Cups	Knight of Swords
Page of Swords	10 of Wands
5 of Swords	7 of Cups
6 of Swords	

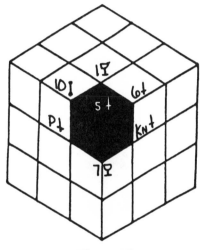

Figure 37

This particular cubic unit shows the influence of four Swords,
one Wand and two Cups. Here the mutable fire of Sagittarius, which
began in the northwest above corner, terminates in the southwest
above corner in the sign of fixed air, Aquarius. Aquarius is the predominant force in this cube. There is, however, a strong influence
from the fixed water sign of Scorpio, rising from the below face of
the cube.

The southwest below cubic unit is bounded on the northeast above and below corner by the Ace of Cups. The northwest above corner is bounded by the Page of Cups and on the below corner by the 4 of Pentacles. The southeast above corner is bounded by the Knight of Pentacles, while the below corner is bounded by the 9 of Cups. The southwest above corner is bounded by the 6 of Cups while the below corner is doubly ruled by the 5 and 10 of Cups.

Ace of Cups	Knight of Pentacles
Page of Cups	4 of Pentacles
9 of Cups	6 of Cups
5 of Cups	10 of Cups

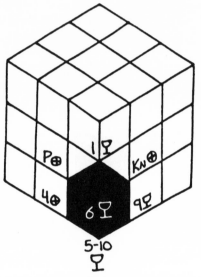

Figure 38

This cubic unit is overwhelmingly influenced by the element of water, both by the fixed sign of Scorpio, and the mutable sign of Pisces. These two signs bring seven Minor Keys to bear on this cube. The remaining influence is from the cardinal sign of Capricorn, which brings its influence from the north to the south, and separates itself by moving either to the surface through the sign of Scorpio or continuing around the below face through the sign of Pisces.

The southeast above cubic unit is bounded on the northwest above and below corners by the Ace of Pentacles.

The northeast above corner is bounded by the 9 of Swords.

The northeast below corner is bounded by the Queen of Swords. The southwest above corner is bounded by the 7 of Swords, while the southwest below corner is bounded by the Knight of Swords. The southeast above corner is bounded by the 8 of Swords, and the southwest below corner is bounded by the 5 of Pentacles.

Ace of Pentacles	Queen of Swords
Knight of Swords	8 of Swords
9 of Swords	7 of Swords
5 of Pentacles	

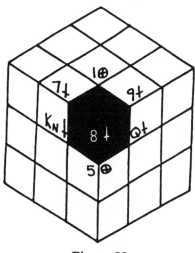

Figure 39

Once again the influence of air is seen through the signs of Gemini and Aquarius, with five Minor Keys in the suit of Swords. The other influence in this cube is that of fixed earth, through the sign of Taurus, with three corners ruled by Pentacles.

The final cubic unit is on the southeast below corner of the Macrocosmic Cube. The northwest above and below corners are bounded by the Ace of Pentacles. The northeast above corner is bounded by the Queen of Pentacles, while the northeast below corner is bounded by the 3 of Cups. The southwest above corner is bounded by the Knight of Cups, and the southwest below corner is held by the 8 of Cups. The southeast above corner is bounded by the 7 of Pentacles, and the southeast below corner is doubly ruled by the 6 of Pentacles and the 4 of Cups.

Ace of Pentacles	Queen of Pentacles
Knight of Cups	3 of Cups
8 of Cups	7 of Pentacles
6 of Pentacles	4 of Cups

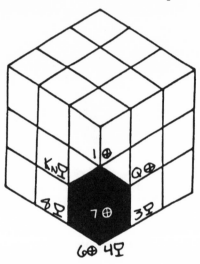

Figure 40

This final cube shows the influence of the element of earth through the five corners ruled by the suit of Pentacles. The fixed sign of Taurus brings the influence from the below to the above face of the cube, and fixes it in consciousness. There are four Minor Keys in the element of water. On the below boundaries of the cube we can see the influence of Pisces flowing from west to east, merging with the influence of Cancer flowing from north to south. There is only one direction in which this influence may flow, and that is through the ascending sign of Taurus.

This completes the definition of the 27 cubic units, as they represent the three axes of the Mother letters and the eight exterior corners.

FOOTNOTES

[1] *DSP,* by Dr. Ann Davies.

CHAPTER SIX

THE MESSAGE OF THE CHALDEAN ORDER

s the study of the Cube of Space grew more involved, I began to get the feeling that there was information that would speak to almost any form of study, whether philosophic, scientific, or spiritual. As models of the Cube were built, I began to see the formation of atoms and elements from the periodic chart. I saw the nesting of geometric forms and the possibilities for new energy devices. My mind began to run wild with ideas of great scientists spending a few minutes looking at a model of the Cube of Space, and gaining a whole new understanding of the cosmologic order through a universal wave theory. Perhaps I became a bit delusional, yet in my heart I feel that there is some truth in the musing I experienced.

My attention then went to the 36 decanates of the Great Zodiacal Wheel. Having spent some time studying it, I began to focus on the combinations of letters that were formed at the various points of the Magic Square of Saturn. Each point on the twelve boundary lines has a merging of two letters of the Aleph-Beth. The combinations become even more complex, when quinances and dwadashamas are considered. These intelligences bring forth messages to those who would take the time to read them. The idea may seem a little fantastic; yet when one approaches the letters as vast beings who have created vehicles of expression in this portion of the universe through the twelve signs of the zodiac and ten planets, we begin to see that they may, indeed, have something to say regarding the creation of the universe and how we may return, in a conscious fashion, to the creative source from whence we came.

The magic of the Minor Arcana does not lie in the use of divination, even though that is a wonderful attribute of the Tarot. The Minor Keys are, indeed, a shorthand symbol system containing the combined influence of the beings of the twenty-two letters of the Chaldean Aleph-Beth. As the different letters come together, there is a harmony or, sometimes, discord that is created. This sets up the environment for something to be experienced in order for humanity to feel the impact of universal forces that aid us in our **Desirous Quest.**[1] They test us, guide us, and instruct us.

THE SIGN OF ARIES

As we have seen in Chapter Four, we are using the Chaldean order of the planets in the planetary attributions of the 36 decanates of the twelve signs of the zodiac. In the sign of Aries, the three planets under consideration are Mars, the Sun, and Venus. These planets are the vehicles set up in this world system for the great beings of Peh, Resh, and Daleth respectively.[2] When these letters are brought in concert with the sign of Aries, and the letter Heh, We have the combinations of:

Peh-Heh, Mars in Aries = 85

Resh-Heh, Sun in Aries = 205

Daleth-Heh, Venus in Aries = 9

The following is a description of how these letters relate.

MARS IN ARIES

  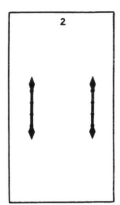

The first consideration is that of Mars/Aries. The Minor Key of the 2 of Wands rests on the northeast corner of the Cube, where the sign of Aries is located. What does this point and all other points on the Cube of Space have to reveal about their influences? Aries is the first sign of the zodiacal cycle, and Mars/Aries is the first decanate of the sign of Aries. There is a total quality of the fiery influence with the cardinal fire of Aries, and the fiery planet Mars. Together they bring forth the **Foundation** of fire. This fiery force is for the construction of necessary forms and the destruction and **Ruin** of forms outworn. This force **Clothes** and **Glorifies** its vessels and brings **Ruin** to that which must be taken away. This force **Impels**, and **Directs** its centers of expression, and brings **Confusion** to the changing vessels. In **Truth**, it is the force that comes from the **Heart of the Stone**[3], which is the heart of the **Lord**.

ISVD - Yesod - Foundation

HOI - Hawi - Ruin

APhD - Ahfad - To Clothe, to Glorify, steadfast

HMM - Hawmam - To Route, to confuse, to impel, to drive.
LB-ABN - Laib ehben - Heart of the Stone

Veritas - Truth

Dominus - Lord

The value of these words is 80, the value of Peh-Heh, Mars in Aries.

THE SUN IN ARIES

The Sun reaches its highest expression in the sign of Aries, and, thus, the 3 of Wands. The combination of these two intelligences brings into balance that which the Master Jesus said was required for peace. "When the Lion (the heart and, thus, the Sun) lies down with the Lamb (the sign of Aries), there will be true peace.

The combined numerical value of these two letters is 205, 200 being the value of Resh, the letter associated with the Sun, and 5 for the letter Heh, associated with Aries.

To truly address the essence of the intelligences combined with the Sun in Aries, one needs to draw their attention to the mountains of attainment in Key number 0, The Fool, Key 6, The Lovers, and Key 8, Strength. This is the same mountain on which the Hermit stands in Key 9, as well as the mountains in the background of Keys 14, Temperance; 17, The Star, and 18, The Moon. The word mountain is the actual combination of the letters of Heh, and Resh (HR), whose values are 205. When one reaches the **Mountain** top, he becomes One with Adam **Qadmon**. He has **Finished** the first part of his journey of becoming "More than Human". He has joined the company of **The Righteous**, and stands with the God from Sinai.

HR - Har - Mountain

H-SLIQ - Ha-Seliq - The End, finished

H-QDVMN - Ha Qadmon - The archetypal man

VTzDQH - Tzedaqah - And the righteous

VIHVH MSINI BA - Jehovah mi Sinai baw - And the God from Sinai.

These words all have a value of 205, the value of the Sun in Aries.

VENUS IN ARIES

  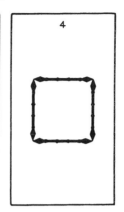

Venus rules the third decanate of Aries and is represented by the 4 of Wands. Its influence is the final tempering of the Mars force that ended the year in Pisces, and began the new year in Aries. There is quite a difference in the temperaments of individuals who are born during the first and third decanates of Aries. Venus brings an opening to the new image, ruled, and organized by the Emperor, Key 4, Aries. This takes place after the destructive fire of Mars destroys the forms outworn. Without the **New Image**, the new form could well be replaced with one even worse than that which is destroyed.

The combined value of Venus in Aries is 9, the letter Daleth=4 the letter Heh=5, 5+4=9. Venus is exalted in the sign of Pisces, which alchemically rules the operation of multiplication. As the multiplying force completes its gestation in the sign of Pisces, it bursts forth in the sign of Aries with the pregnancy of the spring. Ga-Ha (GAH), whose value is 9, means to multiply, to swell or grow.

As the power of creative imagination **Swells** in the spring, there is an anticipation of **Future Growth**, with new forms emerging and **Multiplying**. The **Desire** for creation brings the new form replacing the old, with one form built upon another. There comes forth a knowledge of unity between all things. This knowledge tells us that the **Divine Father, Divine Mother, and Son are One.**

GAH - Ga-Ha - To swell, grow, increase

VBA - Vebaw -Future, coming

VAB - And Father[4]

BDG - Dahg - To multiply abundantly

BAV - In desire

The value of these words are 9, the value of Daleth-Heh, Venus in Aries.

Both the Sun and Mars are at the southern and northern face of the Cube, and are projections of the Holy Mother letter Sheen. Venus is on the eastern end of the axis of Mem. This has been shown in Chapter Four when dealing with the octahedron. Here the first triangle is formed within the Cube of Space, inscribed by the first three decanates of the zodiacal year.

THE SIGN OF TAURUS

Taurus, being the sign of fixed earth, brings a transition from ands to Pentacles, yet continues the order of number and planet, hich was left off in the sign of Aries.

Since 2, 3 and 4 were the numbers in Aries, the 5, 6 and 7 are ose of Taurus. In Aries, the Chaldean order left off with the planet nus. The planet Mercury begins the sign of Taurus.

The Three planets in the sign of Taurus with their corre- onding letters are:

Mercury, Beth, 5 of Pentacles,

Moon, Gimel, 6 of Pentacles,

Saturn, Tav, 7 of Pentacles.

Mercury in Taurus = Vav + Beth = 8

Moon In Taurus = Vav + Gimel = 9

Saturn in Taurus = Vav + Tav = 406

MERCURY IN TAURUS

  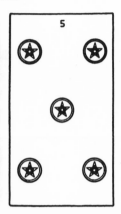

The first planet under consideration in the sign of Taurus is Mercury. It is represented by the 5 of Pentacles. There is a profound relationship between the "Revealer of the Mysteries," Taurus, and Mercury. It is the sign of Taurus that brings the gems of the subconscious mind up into consciousness. The Moon ruling the below face of the Cube, reflects this information into the above face via Taurus, to the Magician/Mercury. It is the path of Taurus, Key 5, The Hierophant, that shows this relationship. In the foreground of Key 5, we see two mendicants in a receptive position, facing the Hierophant; both conscious and subconscious forces are represented. The figure to the left of the Key represents the Alchemical Woman, the figure t the right represents the Alchemical Man. Both are equal in the eyes of the Hierophant.[5]

As true Magicians, we must learn to honor our **Desires**, and acknowledge that they come from the **Seat of Love**. We must **Flow Gently, into that Place,** where we may **Gather Together** the revelations of the **Central Ego.**

> ABH - Ahbaha - To desire
>
> DD - Dad - Seat of love
>
> DBB - Dabab - To flow gently
>
> AZ - Awz - Into that place.
>
> ZA - Notariqon for Zauir Anpin, name for Tiphareth, and the Central Ego.

These words have a value of 8, the value of Mercury in the sign of Taurus.

MOON IN TAURUS

  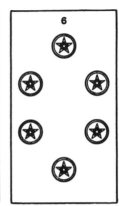

The Moon is the next planet in the Chaldean order. The Moon in Taurus is represented by the 6 of Pentacles. There is an interesting relationship between the Moon in Taurus and Venus in Aries. First of all their values are each 9. Daleth (4) + Heh (5) = 9. Gimel (3) + Vav (6) = 9. The Emperor is the partner of the Empress. They work together in bringing things into manifestation - one, by generating creative images; the other, by organizing the images and setting up the sequence of events necessary to bring the image into physical form.

The High Priestess is the Chief Feminine Elder who represents the Prima Materia of the alchemists. She also holds the records of personal and collective memory. The Heirophant is the agency whereby the memory held by the High Priestess is brought into concious memory and used to generate **New and Improved** suggestions to the subconscious mind.

The alchemical process of circulation is placed into action when these new images are impressed onto the subconscious mind. The subconscious mind then brings forth the new form which in turn generates new images for an even greater refined form. Through this process, the images impressed upon the subconscious mind are congealed through the sign of fixed earth, thus, bringing the first matter into a particular form in the manifested world.

The Prima Materia of the High Priestess is the Invisible Sacred Earth, described by Thomas Vaughn.[6]

This magical earth remains forever **Pure.** It is by **The Power of God** , that **This Water,** gives rise to the **Life** of all creations of **God, Adam, as well as the Devil.** It is through erroneous interpretations and improper suggestions to the subconscious mind, that the concept of **Sin** is born.

> ChI - Chai - Life = 18
>
> ChTA - Khawtaw - Sin, To miss the target.
>
> ZK - Zak - Pure = 27
>
> BKChV - Be-Koakho -By His power = 36
>
> Aqua - Water = 36
>
> ADM - Adam = 45
>
> Homo - Man = 45
>
> Deus - God = 45
>
> Demon - Devil = 45

These words have values which reduce to the number 9, the value of the combined influence of the Moon in Taurus.

SATURN IN TAURUS

  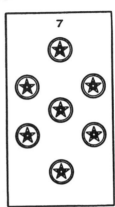

The combination of Saturn and Taurus brings the intention of
e center of the Cube of Space into the fixed earth of Taurus. This is
presented by the 7 of Pentacles. The spelling of the letter Tav is ac-
ally the union of Th+V, or Saturn and Taurus. The letter Tav is at
e end of the Aleph-Beth. There is a sense of completion when
ese two letters combine their influence. With the addition of the
ter Vav at the end of Tav, it tells us that this is the end as well as a
w beginning.

The end and .... This can be seen in Diagram 16 of Chapter 2.
r every ending, there is another beginning.

With the third decanate of Taurus, the central above to below
is of the Cube of Space is defined (See Chapter 4 Figure 11). It
ings agreement to the statement "As above, so below." This axis is
e connecting median between the High Priestess and the Magician
a the internal paths of the Cube. Taurus makes this connection on
e external path of the Cube. Both of the lines of Taurus and Aleph
e parallel. Through the power of Saturn, the Prima Materia of the
igh Priestess is limited by the image sent forth by the self-con-
ious mind.

Through Saturn in Taurus, the One is **Divided** and Spirit **Falls**
to matter, where **The people of the earth** dwell. **Thou** must take up
y **Cross** of manifestation daily, as instructed by the word of **Jesus.**

VPhRSIN - Upharsin - Divided

KShLVN - Kishshawlon - Fall

OM-HARTz- Am-Ha-Eretz- People of the earth

ATvH - Ahtah - Thou

TvV - Tav - Cross

KIShVO - Joshua - Jesus

These words have a value of 406, the value of Saturn in Taurus.

THE SIGN OF GEMINI

The sign of Gemini transfers the elemental quality of Pentacles to that of Swords. This sign holds the influence of the final planet in the Chaldean order and begins the second cycle of the planets
with Mars and the Sun ruling the second and third decanates of
Gemini. Gemini is mutable air and holds the volatile substance of
the air which eludes natural man on earth. It is only through the fixation of the volatile **Spiritus** that the great work can be completed.
This can be seen in both the outward laboratory experiments of the
Alchemists and the inner work of yoga. The letters ruling the decanates of this sign are:

Jupiter- Kaph = 20

Mars - Peh = 80

The Sun- Resh = 200

Gemini- Zain = 7

The 8,9, and 10 of Swords of the Rider Waite deck show some
pretty tragic scenes, which portray the combined influences of
Jupiter, Mars and the Sun in Gemini. This representation of disaster
is more accurately described as the inner experience of separation
from the One into the many. Since the suit of Swords is representative of the Yetziratic World, we can see that the final sense of separation takes place when the astral patterns become concretized in the
world of form. The 10 of Swords represents the vesica that brings astral patterns into the world of form. There is a great opportunity for
transformation with the influences of these planets in the sign of

Gemini. It is the transmutation of the old Yetziratic patterns that hold us in fear and, thus, bondage. We first experience the sense of fear and the image of disaster. Without the transmutation of these patterns, we are left in bondage as seen in Key 15, The Devil.

JUPITER IN GEMINI

  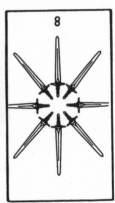

The influence of Jupiter/Kaph coupled with Gemini/Zain adds up to the value of 27. This number has a particular importance because of the 27 cubic units that make up the Cube of Space, through the agency of the Magic Square of Saturn.

There is also a value of 507 when Kaph is considered as a Final letter.

If we consider the current on the boundary line of Taurus on the southeast corner, we can see the influence of Taurus rising and influencing the self-conscious mind in the sign of Gemini. What takes place is the revelation of eternal principles which are reflected from the subconscious mind to the self-conscious mind. The Prima Materia is then discovered and the alchemist may begin the work. The number 27 (KZ) reduces to 9, which is the combined value of the Moon in Taurus (GV). If we were to theosophically extend the number 27 (1+2+3...+27), we would get the number 378. 378 is the number of (ChShML) Khashmal, meaning the instructor of secrets. The sign of Gemini begins with Jupiter. The southeast above corner is the place where Taurus ends and Gemini begins. The mysteries revealed in the sign of Taurus are consciously realized in Gemini.

The Sphere of Jupiter on the Tree of Life is first energized by the 16th Path of Vav, associated with Key 5, The Hierophant. We see is same relationship on the southeast above corner, where the phere of Jupiter receives the influence from the sign of Taurus.

Through the **Revealer of Secrets,** we come to consciously understand the **Serpent** of temptation, and thus come to know the Messiah. We may then enter the **Adytum.** Here, the Son of Man is renewed, as **Shining Gold,** and becomes the **Son of Fire.**

Ka-NChSh - Ka-Nachash - Of the serpent

KMShICh - Ka-Mashshiah - Of the messiah

KBV-AShH - Kaben-Ishshah - Of the son of fire.

ChShML - Khashmal - Shining gold, revealer of secrets

MChVDSh - Mekhodesh - Renewing

All these words have a value of 378, which is the total value of the extension of 27.

MARS IN GEMINI

  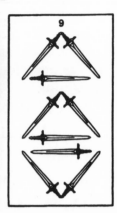

As we move into the second decanate of Gemini and the 9 of Swords, the feeling of separation becomes more intensified. There are a few relationships between Mars and Gemini which need to be addressed. First of all, the sphere of Mars/Severity and the path of Zain proceed from the sphere of Binah/Saturn. Saturn is the secret abode of fire, which in the physical body rests at the base of the spine and is the storehouse of the serpent power. It is the sword of Zain that pierces this sphere and sends the influence from Binah to Tiphareth, sphere of the Sun. After the descent of the path of Zain comes the sphere of Geburah. Geburah, which rests on the pillar of Severity, receives the influence of Binah through the path of Cheth.

Second, as the path of Zain enters the sphere of Tiphareth the path of Heh, Aries, ruled by Mars, descends from Chockmah into Tiphareth. It is at this point that the supernal influence of Chockmah and Binah come together to generate the Son/Sun.

Third, the word Zain, Zain-Yod-Nun, contains the qualities of both the Life Force emanating from the sphere of Chockmah and manifested as the Father through the letter **Yod**, and the vessel of the Mother, in the letter Nun, which represents the 50 gates of Binah.

Fourth, the letter Nun governs the sign of Scorpio, which is ruled by Mars.

Fifth, one can see the contrast between the disaster, resulting from the idea of separation in Key 16, The Tower, symbolized by the two falling figures, and the symbol of right relationship between the masculine and feminine principles, pictured in Key 6, The Lovers.

Our first experience of the transformative influences of Mars/Gemini, the 9 of Swords, is one of fear and **Trembling**.

Through the power **of the Sword** of separation, we come to **Understand** that we are **Vessels,** and centers of **Limitation** for the will of the **All Glorious, Everlasting Father.** The firsthand experience is what the alchemists refer to as **Pure Gold.**

KZLL - Ka-Zahal - To shake or tremble

KZIN - Ka-Zain - Of the sword

K-BINH - Binah - Understanding

ASVK - Awsook - Vessel, flask

BLIMH - Belimah - Limitation

KL-KBVDH - Kahl-kebooddah - All glorious

ABI-OD - Abi - od - Everlasting Father

PhZ - Paz - Pure gold

These words all have a value of 87, the combined value of Mars/Gemini. Note that the word Paz is the actual combination of Peh/Mars and Zain/Gemini.

THE SUN IN GEMINI

  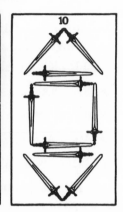

Perhaps the most disheartening picture in the entire Minor Arcana is the one portrayed by the Rider Waite deck, where the aspirant is lying face down on the earth with ten swords stuck in his back, and blood flowing-not a pretty sight. This is perhaps the greatest illusion of fear that is generated by the animal soul. When one decides to really commit to the completion of the Great Work, the first test is one of the fear of death. This fear is usually experienced as simple survival. How will I pay my bills? How will I get what I need to live. This fear is further compounded by those who have not made the choice of completing the Great Work. "Go get a career, you lazy bum!" "You are going to **Die!**" "You will never amount to anything." "That's not the way I raised you!"

Commitment to the Great Work is not an invitation to a life of shirking our responsibilities of living here on earth. We must be in the world but not of it. The Sun/Gemini brings a different reality to bear once we get past the initial illusion. Both the Sun and Archangel Raphael are symbols of alchemical gold, and the sphere of Tiphareth.

The combined value of Resh/Sun and Zain/Gemini is 207. If we bring our attention to the southeastern below corner of the Cube of Space, we can see that the planetary influences of the Moon below, the Sun/south, and Venus/east, have a total value of 207. This influence converges on the southeast corner ruled by the Hierophant, Key 5, Taurus. This intelligence brings these influences into the conscious mind and brings to light the reality that the Lunar and Venusian forces are but reflections of the power which streams from the Sun, and reflects back to the conscious mind superconscious impulses which make the will of the One known. This is vividly pictured in Key 6, The Lovers, associated with the sign of Gemini.

Alchemically the sign of Gemini is associated with the operation of **FIXATION**. This is the fixation of the volatile substance which is the invisible, formless and void earth, spoken of in Genesis and written about by Thomas Vaughn in his *Anthroposophia Theomagica* and his *Magica Adamica*. This volatile substance is present throughout space and can be incorporated in the body through the agency of the blood as it flows through the organ of the lungs.[7]

The Eternal Lord of the Universe, Divided Himself to **Make manifest Forms** of expression within the **Boundless Light**. These vessels are **Refined** so they may be whiteness to the Great **Mystery**, and become a jewel in the **Crown** of the ONE.

ADVN OVLM - Adon Olahm -Eternal Lord of the Universe.

HBR - Habar - To divide, to cut apart

BRH - Barah - To make manifest

GDR - Gadar - Enclosure, form

AYIN-SOPh - Ayin Soph - Boundless, no limit

AUR - Aur - Light, fire

ZQQ - Zaqaq - Refine, to strain, to filter

RZ - Raz - Mystery

ZR - Zare - Crown, border, necklace

The value of these words are 207, the value of Zain + Resh. Note that the words crown and mystery are the exact combination of Zain and Resh.

The Sign of Cancer

The final sign in the first quarter of the zodiacal year is Cancer. It is the movement from the spring equinox to the summer solstice. The current of Cancer and the letter Cheth take the influence from the conscious mind, as it descends through the current of Aries, and brings it through the subconscious level to the sign of Taurus where the subconscious mind reflects back to the conscious mind the wisdom of superconsciousness. There is a circulation process that could go on forever due to the clockwise flow of energy on the eastern face of the Cube. This is a reversal of the flow of currents that move on the above face of the Cube which moves in a counterclockwise direction.

The eastern face of the Cube works with both modes of personal consciousness. The creative images are formed in the eastern face through the planet Venus and the letter Daleth which occupies the eastern face. These images are then organized by The Emperor, the sign of Aries, and the letter Heh. The suggestion is then firmly planted in the subconscious mind by the descent of the letter Heh, and is worked upon by the forces of the subconscious mind through the agency of the letter Cheth. The results are brought back to the conscious mind so that there may be a building on the product of the first suggestion to create more refined images. Round and round it goes. It is through this process that we learn from our mistakes and are able to create a world of peace.

The three decanates of Cancer are ruled by Venus, Mercury and the Moon. Their letter values are:

Venus-Daleth = 4

Mercury-Beth = 2

Moon-Gimel = 3

Cancer-Cheth = 8

VENUS IN CANCER

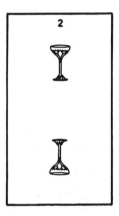

Venus in Cancer is the result of the path of Daleth as it oscil-
es between the sphere of Chockmah and the sphere of Binah. It is
presented by the 2 of Cups. The path of Cheth descends from the
th of Binah after being influenced by the path of Daleth. The path
Cheth takes this influence and pours it into the pillar of Severity.

Venus in Cancer is also the result of the things that began in
 conscious mind in the sign of Aries. The suggestions given to the
oconscious mind are now in the process of being made manifest
form, through the agency of Cancer. This process can be plainly
tnessed in nature. The seeds planted in the spring/Aries take
ar form in the summer/Cancer. Key 3, The Empress, shows the
undance of nature, in the field of operation/Cheth when the prop-
seeds are planted.

In the 2 of Cups, we can experience the right relationship be-
een the masculine and feminine forces, which are rightly seen in
 line of Gemini, Key 6, The Lovers. This line lies directly above
d is parallel with the line of Cancer. (east above, The Lovers, and
st below, Cancer).

The planting of one seed will result in the multiplication of its
d. When properly cared for and cultivated, the One brings forth

the many, and from this many, a few will bring forth the next generation. One kernel of corn will produce the entire ear which will have hundreds of kernels. Some of these kernels will be eaten by insects, some will rot, and some will be planted for next year's harvest.

The combinations of Keys 3, The Empress, and 7 The Chariot, show the process of multiplication through the relationship between the numbers 7 and 12. When the Emperor, Key 4, brings the influence of self-consciousness to bear on Key 3, creative imagination, the result is a field of operation shown by Key 7, 3+4=7. In the more sublime worlds, this process brings forth the 7 sacred planets.

When the forces of 3 and 4 are multiplied, we have the 12 centers of expression known as the signs of the zodiac. The value of the letter Cheth is 8. Cheth combined with Daleth, 4 = 12. Through the powers of the **One**, its centers of expression receive the impulse to **Grow and Multiply**. The impulse to do so is experienced as a **Wish** or **Desire**. The will to create brings a great **Treasury of Riches** to the center of expression. At all times, the center of expression and the One are joined together through the agency of **(Vav) The Nail or Hook.**

> HVA - Hu - Name for God.[8]
>
> DGH - Dwagh - To grow and multiply
>
> AVH - Avah - To wish for
>
> Gaza (from the Greek) - Treasury, riches.
>
> VV - Vav - Nail or hook.

These words all have a value of 12, the same value as that of Venus/Cancer.

MERCURY IN CANCER

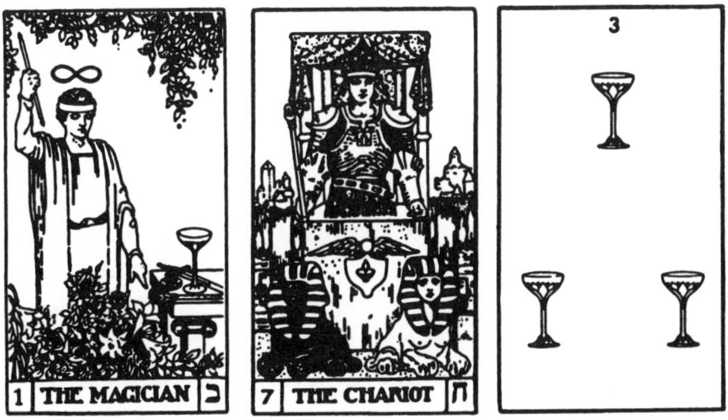

Alchemically, Cancer is the operation of Separation. The para-x of separation is the major theme throughout all the western ysteries. It is perhaps the greatest paradox we are faced with as as-rants. The reality of separation and unity are continually present. e combination of Mercury and Cheth, symbolized by the 3 of ps, shows us a few representations of the mystery of separation.

First, the 3 of Cups is the manifestation of the limiting power Saturn through the third Sephiroth of Binah. What is being limit- here is the creative image-making power in the world of Briah, e world of creative ideas. What is being separated is one specific ea from the infinite storehouse of ideas. Without a specific creative age, 2 of Cups, Venus in Cancer, we cannot fix the Prima Materia at exists at the subconscious level on the below face of the Cube. ence, the 3 of Cups, Mercury in Cancer, maintains the creative in-ntion that originated on the self-conscious level as it circulates on e below face of the Cube.

Second, the letter Beth is the first letter of Genesis. Its mean-g is **HOUSE**. It creates a boundary between the formless and void d that which has form. So we read in Genesis 1:1 "In the Begin-ng the creative powers **SEPARATED** the heavens from the earth." e first separation was that which is above from that which is be-w, and that which is without from that which is within.

As separation is the major theme of our evolution, so Beth sets the vessel, for the sake of separation, where a center of expression ay reside. What is being evolved? The personalities of the centers expression. Where do these centers of expression find a place to olve? In the field of Cheth. The field is the place where the stage is set. Experience bears the true knowledge that although we are most certainly centers of expression with unique roles to play in the Mind of the All, we are at no time separated from the Will of the One.

The value of Mercury/Beth and Cancer/Cheth is 10. Beth (2) + Cheth (8) = 10. In the Tarot series, Beth is attributed to Key 1, The Magician, and 1 is the same value as the theosophical reduction of the number 10 (10 = 1 + 0 = 1). As the number 1 is the beginning of the numerical series, so Beth is, **In the beginning,** of the story of creation.

Cheth is attributed to Tarot Key 7. 7 when extended, 1 + 2 + 3... + 7 = 28 (2 + 8 = 10), and (1 + 0 = 1). As Beth is the first vessel, so Cheth is the first arena where the first vessel may find its place of expression. This is intimated on the 12th and 18th paths of the Tree of Life. Beth first descends from Kether and energizes the sphere of Binah. From Binah, Cheth descends into the sphere of Geburah, the sphere of Divine Will.

The first appearance of the letter Cheth in Genesis is Genesis 1:2, in the word ChShK-Khoshek, Darkness. This is the darkness of the below face of the Cube. The next appearance of the letter Cheth is in the word RVCH-Ruach, Spirit. It is this spirit which hovers above the dark. This is the power of self-consciousness via the line of Gemini, ruled by Mercury, hovering over the darkness of the line of Cancer.

It is the work of the **Magician** to recognize the **Unity** of all things, even though the outer appearance is one of **Separation.** Through the **Window** of our senses, we feel **Divided.** Through the power of attention, we may discover the **Hiding Place** of the One.

> AT - Ate - Magician
>
> AHD - Ohad - Unity, to unite
>
> BDD - Bawdahd - Separation
>
> HH - Heh - Window
>
> BZA - Bawzah - To divide
>
> ChB - Khobe - Hiding place

These words all have a value of 10, the value of Cheth/Beth.

THE MOON IN CANCER

  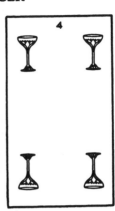

Where Mercury in Cancer is the combination of influences of the above face of Mercury and the below east line of Cancer, the Moon in Cancer is the influence of the below face of the Cube, symbolized by the 4 of Cups. This is the place of transition where the Prima Materia enters into a field of activity/Cheth. There is a dual purpose here for the vehicle of the Chariot. First, as already explained, the vehicle of Cheth brings creative images originating in self-consciousness, through the below face, so that these images of suggestion may be harvested in the manifested world. Second, the subconscious mind is also the reflective quality where superconciousness is revealed to self-consciousness. The Chariot, Key 7, then is the vehicle which delivers superconscious intelligence to self-conciousness. Before the wisdom of the High Priestess, Key 2 can be revealed, it must traverse the east below line of Cancer and ascend through the line of Taurus. It is here that the Moon moves from rulership in Cancer to exaltation in Taurus. Both the Magician and the Empress are represented in Key 5, as they kneel in a receptive position, showing their equal standing before the revealer of the mysteries. The exalted quality of the High Priestess/Moon is the revelation of the mysteries to the self-conscious mind.

The total value of The High Priestess/Gimel and the value of The Chariot/Cheth, is 11. Eleven is the value of AVD-Ode, the Fire of the Magic of Light. This is the substance that has been recognized as the emanating force from all things.[9]

The word (DLTh) door, whose value is 434 reduces to the number 11, the value of (GCh). The combination of the letters of Daleth represent the astrological influences of the sign of Libra, its ruling planet Venus, and its exalted planet Saturn. The influence of the 4 of Cups can rise either into the line attributed to Taurus or through Final Kaph which ascends from the southeast below corner to the northwest above corner. When the 4 of Cups rises through Final Kaph, it comes in contact with the powers of Daleth. It is here that contact is made with the line of Libra which may bring the influence of the 4 of Cups back to the below face to meet the dweller on the threshold in the sign of Capricorn.

At the southeast below corner, there is a double ruling of the Moon. The 4 and 6 of Cups are both placed there. These represent the Moon in Cancer, and the Moon in Taurus. This brings together the influence of Taurus (Vav), Cancer (Cheth), and the Moon (Gimel). These same letters are the paths on the Tree of Life which descend from the supernal triad of Kether, Chockmah, and Binah. These paths flow into the three pillars of the Tree of Life, Mercy, Severity and Mildness. Gimel descends from Kether to form the Pillar of Mildness or the Middle Pillar. Vav descends from Chockmah into the Pillar of Mercy, while Cheth descends into the Pillar of Severity, from the sphere of Binah. The total letter value is 17. This is the value of DIV - Dehyo, the fluid darkness. This is the state of the Prima Materia as it exists on the below face of the Cube. The word "hovering", (MRChPhTh) Merachepth, Genesis 1:2 has a value of 728, which reduces to 17, the value of VChG. The word hovering brings us back to the sign of Gemini which hovers above the sign of Cancer. Ruach Elohim (RVCh ELHIM), whose value is 300, is the spirit of God mentioned in Genesis, as hovering above the waters (Cancer). Ruach is the airy spirit attributed to Gemini. The value of the planetary triad that rules the three decanates of Gemini is 300, the value of Ruach Elohim. It is the influence of self-consciousness on the above face that directs the fluid darkness into becoming a particular form of expression. The 3 of Cups is that self-conscious influence. Self-consciousness riding in the Chariot, (Beth+Cheth), Mercury in Cancer, through the fluid darkness (Moon in Cancer).

By means of the influence of the 4 of Cups, the aspirant may drink from the infinite **Reservoir** of the subconscious mind, and **Separate the Prima Materia** from its **Vapor** state so that it may **Bear Fruit.** In doing so, the **Gate** is opened to the **Upper Surface** of the Cube of Space where we may **Behold the Secret Magical Fire,** revealed by the Father and Mother.

HAGB - Hagab - The means by

HGBA - Hagehbeh - The reservoir

BD - H-Bad - Separated

V-AD - Vade - Vapor, mist[10]

VABB - Va-Ahbab - And to bear fruit, to blossom.

VBBA - Vabahbah - Gate, door

VGB - Vagab - Upper surface

HHA - Ha-Heh - To behold

AVD - Ode - The fire of the magic light.

These words have a value of 11, the value of the Moon in Cancer.

This completes the formation of the eastern face of the Cube. These are the northeastern corner of Aries, the southeastern corner of Taurus, the east above line of Gemini, and the east below line of Cancer. These lines take us through the spring to the beginning of the summer, and from the formless and void state to the formed state.

THE SIGN OF LEO

Cancer is the vehicle for the expression of the lunar intelligence on the below face of the Cube. Leo is the means of expression of the solar intelligence on the above face of the cube.

After one circulates on the eastern face of the Cube, the experience of the deep may be integrated on the conscious level of the upper surface of the Cube. Here, what has begun in the east flows to the west through the line of Leo along the north above line of the Cube.

Leo is the second fiery sign in the zodiacal year. The fire of Leo is a fixed fire. The fire of Aries is a cardinal fire. What is initiated in the sign of Aries is brought into fixation in the sign of Leo.

In the sign of Leo, the Sun is the ruler with the planet Neptune exalted. This is the first outward appearance of an outer planet, or Mother Letter, in the zodiacal year. In the first fire sign, Aries, we see the exaltation of the Sun. In the second fire sign, Leo, we find the rulership of the Sun.

There is an important connection between the intelligence of Aries and the intelligence of Leo. First Aries descends from the sphere of Chockmah, the sphere of the Divine Father, connecting with the sphere of Tiphareth. Chockmah, the Father, connects with the Son/Sun. What is the highest expression or exaltation of the Sun in Aries? It is the physical embodiment of the Divine Father through the agency of the Divine Son. The mystery of this projection, of the essence of spirit into form, is perhaps one of the greatest clues for the understanding of fourth dimensional consciousness. The initiating, or cardinal principle of the Father finds expression in the physical form of the Son. In the sign of Leo, the Father is fixed in the

Sun/Son. This idea once again is expressed in the Stone of the Wise. ABN-Ehben-Stone, AB-Father, BN-Son; the Father and Son are One.

The sign of Leo is the sign for the tribe of Judah, IHVDH. This was the tribe of Jesus, who was called the Son of God by the Christian faith. Furthermore, the concept of the Father and the Son being One is brought forth in the concept of the Lion and the Lamb lying down together, Leo and Aries. Gad (GD) is the tribe associated with the sign of Aries. Its value is 7. The value of (IHVDH) is 30. The combined value of 37 is the value of (IChIDH) Yehkidah, the Central Self, centered in all creation, and attributed to the sphere of Kether. When Final Nun is considered as 700, the value of Ehben is 703, which is the extension of the number 37, 1+2+3+4...+37 = 703.

The three planets in the Leo triplicity are:

Saturn - Tav - 400

Jupiter - Kaph - 20

Mars - Peh - 80

SATURN IN LEO

The sign of Leo is the first sign that begins its decanate series with the sphere of Binah, the first of the planetary spheres on the Tree of Life. The only other sign to begin with Saturn is that of Pisces.

Saturn and Leo, represented by the 5 of Wands, bring together the influence of the limiting power of Saturn (which is the secret abode of fire) with the sign of Leo, fixed fire. Leo is the place where the secret fire is released as it moves throughout the spinal column and nerve centers. After much work, this power energizes the seven sacred planets called chakras, where the coiled one weaves itself around the spinal caduceus.

Saturn and Leo are further connected through their letter symbols. The letter Teth is the serpent power; Tav is the secret abode of this power. The ancient symbol for the letter Tav is the cross. The symbol for Teth was a circle around a cross. The circle is also a symbol of the serpent biting its tail.[11]

Without the limiting power of Saturn, the secret fire would have no vessel to work in and, hence, no manifestation.

In Key 21, The World, we see the cosmic dancer holding this serpent power in spiral forms. One is ascending, the other descending. This same force is seen in symbolism in Key 8, Strength, above the head of the alchemical woman in the form of the figure 8. There is also a figure 8 around the lion and the woman in a chain of roses.

The 5 of Wands expresses these two influences, and offers the opportunity for the purification of the alchemical water, symbolized by the exaltation of Neptune in Leo.

There is yet another strong connection between the letters Teth and Tav. Just as the primitive letter Tav is inscribed by the circle of Teth, so the combined influences of Teth and Tav, which add up to 409, are seen in the root of the letter Teth when it is spelt in full (TTh), a value of 409.[12]

Through the limiting power of Saturn, **the Boundless Limitless Light Brings Forth the Azoth** to operate within fixed vehicles the **Serpent** power.

H-AYIN SVPh AVR - Ayin Soph Aur - The limitless light

H-MShVTTIM - Mashottim - The going forth

H-AZVTh - Azoth - Name for the first matter

TITh - Teth - Serpent

These words have a value of 419, the full spelling of Teth, when Teth is spelled (TITh).

JUPITER IN LEO

  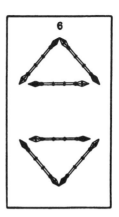

The 6 of Wands brings an opposite quality of Saturn to the sign of Leo. The limiting quality of Saturn makes way for the expansive quality of Jupiter. Before the expansive intelligence of Jupiter can be made manifest, there must be limits set by Saturn. It is the Magic Square of Saturn which gives rise to the Cube of Space that we are considering here. The next Magic Square to be generated from the Magic Square of Saturn is that of Jupiter, whose number is 16. (See Chapter 2 Figure 16).

Just as Aries and Leo are connected in their relationship to the Sun, so Pisces and Leo are connected through their relationship to Neptune, The Hanged Man. Their relationship is further enforced by the intelligence of Jupiter and the letter Kaph. Jupiter is the co-ruler of Pisces with Neptune. Jupiter also rules the second decanate in Leo. Kaph/Jupiter is also the final diagonal which connects Pisces and Leo on the Cube of Space. Final Kaph travels from the end of Pisces at the southeast below corner through the center of the Cube and intersects the northwest above corner terminating at Leo.

The major relationship between the letters Teth and Kaph, Jupiter/Leo, is through the traverse path of Teth on the Tree of Life, which connects the sphere of Jupiter to that of Mars. The path of Teth brings the intelligence of Chesed in balance with that of Geburah.

There is another connection between the intelligence of Jupiter in Leo. This is seen on the Cube of Space on the line of Leo which terminates on the western face, governed by Jupiter and the letter Kaph.

From Everlasting to everlasting, **The One, Declares** himself to all centers of expression.

H-MQDM MIMI OVLM - Miqqedem Mimay Olahm - From everlasting

H-MSPhRIM - Mesaperiym - Declaration

H-NPhSh - Nephesh - Animal soul

H-SPhR MIM - Sepher M - The Book of Moses

These words have a value of 435, the extension of the letters Kaph and Teth, 20+9=29. 1+2+3+4...+29=435.

MARS IN LEO

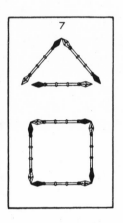

Mars in Leo, the 7 of Wands, is in some ways the product of the first two decanates of Leo. As the Magic Square of Jupiter is generated from the square of Saturn, so the square of Mars follows the square of Jupiter, (see Chapter 2, Figure 16).

The relationships between Mars, Jupiter, and Leo continue to unfold. Once again, we can refer to the path of Teth, which balances the two planetary spheres of Mars and Jupiter on the Tree of Life. The line of Leo on the Cube of Space transverses the northern face of Mars and terminates on the western face of Jupiter. The Magic Square of Jupiter is 16, the same as the number of the Tarot Key attributed to Mars, The Tower.

The letter Peh, is associated with the Life Force, seated in Chockmah. It finds manifestation as the electric currents in our blood and nervous system, as well as the force which fires our desire nature.

The combined symbols of The Tower/Mars, and Strength/Leo, speak to the need to purify our desire nature.

Our **Physical Bodies,** are vehicles of expression of the Divine. We must **Cast out** all **Illusions** that personal will originates within us. By piercing the **Veil** of **Illusion,** we will come **To Know** the **Soul of the World.**

GVPh - Guph - The physical body.

HDPh - Hadaph - To cast out.

LTIM - Lataim - Illusions.

ChPhA - Khahfah - To cover, To veil.

IHDY - Yawda - To see, to know.

Anima Mundi - Soul of the world.

These words have a value of 89, the same value as Peh/Teth, Mars in Leo.

THE SIGN OF VIRGO

As Leo brought the information received by the conscious mind from the east to the west, so the sign of Virgo and Key 9, The Hermit, bring the automatic response of subconsciousness from east to west. What does it mean to bring that which began in the east to the west in relationship to the sign of Virgo? Since the sign of Virgo resides on the north below line of the Cube of Space, we can say that the operation in Virgo is in the subconscious domain. In the sign of Leo, we see the alchemical woman taming the red lion. This is symbolic of control to the response of the animal soul. In the sign of Virgo, this response generates new automatic responses on the subconscious level that are parallel with the conscious work taking place in the sign of Leo. This happens in a twofold way.

First, the work on the conscious level brings new suggestions into the subconscious mind and thus changes the **Response** of the **Vital Soul** to outer forms of stimulation. Our appetites, whether for food, drink, or sex become more regulated. Instead of being dragged by the wild horses of our senses, one becomes master of them.

Second, there is an environment which is set up where the cellular consciousness of our corporate being is transformed through the small intestine, ruled by Virgo.[13]

The key word then for Key 9 is response. When our animal soul is under direct control within our personal vehicle by the Central Ego, we then respond to that Ego in a clear unfailing way, which brings right action into our life.

THE SUN IN VIRGO

  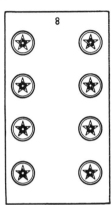

The 8 of Pentacles represents the combined forces of the Sun in Virgo, as these forces exist within the sphere of intellect, Hod. This combination of the letters Resh and Yod represent the releasing of the **Potable Gold** of the alchemists. This takes place in the small intestine where the white milky substance, chyle, is absorbed by the lacteals. The small intestine is ruled by Virgo.

The Sun has long been associated with the completion of the Great Work. For it is our solar logos, which is the **Word/Logos,** spoken of in the Gospel of Saint John. In alchemy, the Sun is a symbol of **gold,** and both bear the same alchemical symbol. The combined value of Resh/Yod is 210, which is the extension of the number 20. The 20th path is the path of Yod, the path of The Hermit, which is ruled by Virgo.

If we bring our attention to the 26th path of Ayin, we find The Devil connecting the path of Hod to the sphere of the Sun. It is our lower mind which creates the phantoms of illusion, which distorts the divine impulse and creates fear in the heart of the aspirant. If we look beyond The Devil, through the sphere of Tiphareth, we see the lantern of The Hermit shining forth from the 20th path.

When the power of the Sun is released in the body of the aspirant, the gift of **Vision,** is received. The great **Treasury,** is seen through the **Window** of the eye, and will behold the radiant **Fluid Darkness,** set into form by the **Hand** of God.

> IVD - Yod - Hand
>
> AChVH - Akhavah - Declaration
>
> DIV - Deyo - Fluid darkness

HH-HH - Heh - Window

HIH - Hiyah - To Make

ChZH - Khawzah - To see, prophet, vision

H'gaza - The treasury (Greek).

These words have a value of 20, the number when extended equals 210, the combined value of Yod and Resh.

Words with a value of 170 are: LOINI - Thine eyes

MLPhNI - From thy presence

TzDIP - Righteous = 184

VENUS IN VIRGO

  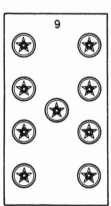

As the Sun in Virgo brings the potable gold of the alchemists into the bloodstream of the aspirant, so Venus in Virgo, the 9 of Pentacles, brings forth the creative image that allows this release to take place.[14] Virgo is the sign of the Virgin. The alchemists say, **"Dame Venus comes to her wooers in foul garments."** Without going into details, we can safely say that the small intestine, though vital for both physical existence and spiritual transformation, has some foul aspects. Yet this area of the body, ruled by the sign of Virgo, is brought into exalted function by the creative images generated through the letter Daleth, The Empress, and the planet Venus. The combined intelligences of Venus in Virgo create a relationship between the eastern, northern, and below faces of the Cube.

The eastern face brings a new beginning through the power of creative imagination. The north face brings into play the vital Life

ce, **Chiah.** The planet Mars is the agent of the Life Force. The be-
face takes the powers of the subconscious symbolized by the
h Priestess, and brings forth the regenerated body of the Adept.

The simple spelling of the letter Yod, the creative hand of
n, is the combination of the intelligences of Venus in Virgo,
l/Daleth. Their combined value is 14. The extended value of 14 is
the Latin value for **Genus Homo-The Human Race,** and **Meas**
toria- My Victory.

If one is to really take on the Great Work, there must be the
lingness for **Sacrifice.** All things which stand in the way must be
noved. When we stretch forth our **Hand,** we will be greeted by the
oved One Who is **Pierced and Separated,** for the sake of creation.

HBHB - Habhahb - Sacrifice

ID - Yod - Hand.

DVD - David - beloved

ATD - Ahtahd - Pierced

ese words have the value of 14, the combined value of Daleth/Yod.

MERCURY IN VIRGO

  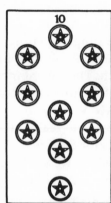

In the entire zodiacal series, there is only one planet which is both ruler and exalted in the same sign. This takes place in the sign of Virgo with the planet Mercury, symbolized by the 10 of Pentacles. Virgo, the north below line on the Cube, is specifically a subconscious process. The presence of Mercury, both as ruler and exalted planet, reminds us that the subconscious is amenable to suggestion from acts of intention originating in the self-conscious mind. Through the proper suggestions, the self-conscious mind may direct the powers inherent in the sign of Virgo, thus creating a regenerated physical body. This is accessing what the alchemists call **Sophic Mercury**.

In the area of rulership, Mercury is the house, the personal ego, as well as the physical body, which needs to be transmuted. In the exalted state, Mercury is the temple/house of the Lord, which is **"MADE WITHOUT HANDS."** This is where the aspirant has attained the state of being, symbolic of the picture in Key 9, The Hermit.

The 10 of Pentacles, in combination with the 9 of Pentacles, brings self-consciously (Mercury) directed images (Venus) into operation within the Virgo region of the body to create the transmuted body of the Adept.

When the powers of Sophic Mercury direct the subconscious forces, the **Mezla**, in the form of chyle, **Drips** into the blood stream. When this takes place in the House of **Bread (Bethlachem)**, there is a sublime **Salt** which allows the **Binding** of the volatile elements in the atmosphere, thus **Initiating** the aspirant into the fifth Kingdom.

MZLA - Mezlah - Holy Influence, to drip, to flow, radiant energy.

LChM - Lechem - Bread

ChLM - Ckholem - To bind

ChNK - Enoch - Initiated

ese words have a value of 78, which is the extended value of the
nbined values of Mercury in Virgo, Beth/Yod.

This completes the first half of the zodiacal year. In a sense,
zodiacal forces have been brought into play, for when one energy
activated, its compliment is always brought into activity as well.

The next chapter will conclude with the last six signs looking
ther into the letter/number combinations of the signs and plan-
as they whirl around the boundaries of the Cube of Space.

FOOTNOTES

[1] The Desirous Quest is the intelligence attributed to the letter Kaph which is the 21st path on the Tree of Life, and the planetary force of Jupiter, that resides on the western face of the Cube of Space.

[2] *The Power of Aleph,* by Philip S. Berg.

[3] The Heart of the Stone is in reference to the Philosophers Stone symbolic of the sphere of Tiphareth, the central Ego. The word Eben (ABN), meaning stone in Hebrew, contains the words (AB) Father, and (BN) Son, "The Father and the Son are One"

[4] VAB, is a special spelling for the Father and Notariqon for Aima, and Ben, son. This refers to the Father, Mother, and Son as being One.

[5] *The Tarot,* by Dr. Paul Foster Case.

[6] Thomas Vaughn writes of the magical and invisible earth in his *Anthroposophia Theomagica* and his *Magica Adamica.*

[7] Dr. Paul Foster Case, *The Great Work*

[8] The name Hu is representative of the aspect of God that is unmanifest and continually directs and images centers of expression.

[9] *The Magical Language* by Paul Foster Case.

[10] This word is representative of the Prima Materia in its formless and void state on the lower face of the Cube.

[11] *The Book of Tokens* by Dr. Paul Foster Case. Comment on Teth.

[12] This is the spelling used by Fabre D'Olivet in his *Hebraic Tongue Restored.* It is a root word in Arabic. In *Godwin's Cabalistic Encyclopedia,* the letter Teth is spelled TITh, which would give a value of 419.

[13] Dr. Case speaks about this process throughout the curriculum in the lessons of the B.O.T.A.

[14] These ideas come from the writings of Dr. Paul Foster Case.

CHAPTER SEVEN

THE SIGN OF LIBRA

he sign of Libra is the beginning of the second half of the zodiacal year. As the beginning of the year began with the vernal equinox, so the second half begins with the autumnal equinox.

On the Tree of Life, the 22nd path of Lamed, attributed to Libra and Key 11, Justice, connects the sphere of Volition (Geburah) with the Central Ego in Tiphareth.

On the Cube of Space, the path of Libra and the letter Lamed takes the influence from the sign of Leo and directs it into the below face of the Cube, where its influence is picked up by the sign of Capricorn.

The Faithful Intelligence assigned to Libra, is tested as the current descends and meets the Dweller on the Threshold, The Devil.

The picture in Key 11 shows the alchemical woman holding things in balance. Balance is what occurs in the mixture of day and night at the moment of the equinox.

One of the several occult dictums states, "Equilibration is the secret of the great work". When our various bodies are brought into balance, that is, mental, emotional and physical, we are in a space to be receptive to the clear directive teachings of the Divine Will.

The planet Venus is the ruling intelligence of Libra and indicates that the power of creative imagination is the means of transmuting karma.

Saturn is the planet exalted in Libra and teaches us the proper application of limitation in our creative imaging.

As with all other astrological signs, there is a particular theater set up within a specific sign where the planetary forces may bring forth their influence.

The letter Lamed (LMD) means ox goad as a noun, and "to teach" as a verb having the same numerical value as the words:

DIIN – Diin – Leader, Chief, Judge

ISD – Yawsad – Law.

(Libra then, is the sign set apart as the teacher, judge, and director of The One Life's myriad centers of expression.)

As we saw the Chaldean order begin with Mars in the sign of Aries, so we see this order come to completion in the sign of Libra. The planetary intelligences attributed to the decanates of Libra are:

The Moon – Gimel – 3

Saturn – Tav – 400

Jupiter – Kaph – 20

THE MOON IN LIBRA

  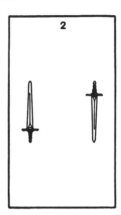

The Moon in Libra is represented by the 2 of Swords. The suit of Swords represents the Yetziratic world, where the astral mind stuff is congealed into a specific form, where it becomes manifested in the world of Assiah.

Since Libra is associated with karma, we can see the law of karma come into play as the sign of Libra descends into the below face of the Cube. Libra is located on the northwest corner. As it descends, it brings its influence to the below face where it comes into the domain of the High Priestess, the subconscious mind, ruled by the Moon.

We can ask ourselves, what is karma? It is actually the Hermetic Law of Cause and Effect. The law is stated, "Every Cause has its Effect; every Effect has its Cause; everything happens according to Law; Chance is but a name for Law not recognized; there are many planes of causation, but nothing escapes the Law." Whatever suggestions we present to the subconscious mind, we bring the law of Cause and Effect into play. This is karma, plain and simple.

When the line of Libra takes self-conscious suggestions back into the subconscious mind, ruled by the Moon, we can adapt and change the astral patterns that create the uncomfortable situations we are faced with in the present.

The Moon in Libra is a symbol of bringing our actions into balance with the laws of the universe.

The value of the Moon/Gimel, in Libra/Lamed, is 33. Thirty-three is the number of the Master Teacher. When the mind stuff of the below face of the Cube has congealed into a particular manifestation in the world of form, we are forced and guided to learn and refine our creative powers.

The Prima Materia is forever **Clean and Pure.** It is like the **Clay** of the earth. Through the **Power** of suggestion, the clay takes form. From within the **Nothing**, the **Clay** of the earth comes forth, fulfilling the will in **God**, thy **Father** .

V-ZK - Zak - Clean and pure

H-TIT - Ha-Tiyt - The clay

H-KCh - Ha-Kokh - The power

BLA - BLO - The nothing

BAL - Bel - In god

ABIK - Abika - Thy father

These words have a value of 33, the value of Gimel/Lamed.

SATURN IN LIBRA

  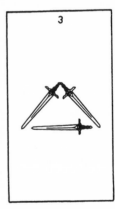

The intelligence of Saturn in Libra is represented by the 3 of Swords. The Waite deck uses the symbol of the heart pierced by three swords. This is the **Vision of Sorrow** attributed to the sphere of Binah. The 3 of Swords is seated in the sphere of Binah as are all other Minor Keys bearing the Number 3.

Since Binah is the sphere of Saturn, the 3 of Swords holds a unique relationship with the third Sephiroth. The other Minor Keys holding the Number 3 are ruled by different planetary intelligences. The 3 of Wands is ruled by the Sun in Aries, the 3 of Cups is ruled by Mercury in Cancer, and the 3 of Pentacles is ruled by Mars in

Capricorn. Since the sphere of Binah holds the same planetary influence as that of the 3 of Swords, the sense of separation becomes more apparent. The 3 of Swords then speaks to the limiting power of Saturn through the process of separation. This is accomplished by limiting our creative images. Remember that Venus rules creative imagination as well as the sign of Libra where Saturn is exalted. Furthermore, it is Venus that unites the sphere of the Divine Father with the sphere of the Divine Mother.

On the northwest line of Libra, the intelligence of Saturn moves from the exalted state in Libra into ruling the sign of Capricorn. This phenomenon has been dealt with at some length:

As the intelligences of a particular planetary influence play through a particular zodiacal sign, the environment is set up for this type of change. Furthermore, we can begin to see subtle relationships established between the signs of rulership and the signs of exaltation of a particular planet.

As the exalted Saturn descends the northwest line of Libra, it takes with it the transmuted **Animal Soul**, seen in Key 8 of Leo, and is tested by the Dweller on the Threshold, **The Devil**. There the **Invisible Earth** which has been **Concealed**, will be shown to thee.

NPhSh - Nefesh - The animal soul

Demon + OShIH - The demon of the manifested world

ThHV VBHV - Tohu va-Bohu - Formless and void

ShPhN - Shfan - Concealed

These words have a value of 430, the combined influence of Saturn in Libra, Tav/Lamed.

JUPITER IN LIBRA

  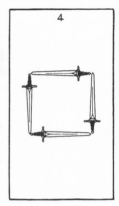

Since the line of Libra binds the northern and western faces of the Cube, we can see the direct relationship to the line of Libra and the planet Jupiter which is assigned to the western face of the Cube, and symbolized by the 4 of Swords.

As already discussed in Chapter 6, the final diagonal of Kaph ascends from the southeast below corner through the center and then terminates at the northwest above corner. The influence of Final Kaph travels in two directions. The above current takes Final Kaph and sends it along the line of west above ruled by the letter Samek and the sign of Sagittarius. Jupiter, as we know, is ruler of this sign.

The second option of energy flow is through the sign of Libra, already mentioned. There is a circulation of the influence of Final Kaph on the above to the below faces.

The 4 of Swords brings forth the personal memory about past experiences, which lead to the present situations.

Through the intelligence of Jupiter in Libra, **Humanity** can know what course of action is necessary to confront the **Devil**, see beyond our **Fears**, and transmute our **Pains and Sorrows**, into the **Abundance** of our birthright as children of Majesty.

H-ADM - Ha-Adam - Generic humanity

H-ZZAL - Ha-Zazel - The spirit of Saturn[1]

ChBLI -Khobli - Pains and sorrows

ZCHL - Zakhal - To fear

H-HM - HaHem - The abundance

hese words have a value of 50, the combined value of Kaph/Lamed, piter in Libra.

Looking for the hidden relationships between zodiacal and lanetary intelligences can create a whole new way of understand- ng astrology. If we brought our attention to Chapter 6, we would e that the signs of Aries and Taurus occupy corners of the Cube of pace which are opposite in direction. Aries is on the northeast cor- er, and Taurus on the southeast corner. Aries is ruled by Mars, Tau- is is ruled by Venus.

We now come into the opposite time of the year where we nd the sign Libra opposite Aries. Instead of north to south their re- tionship is east to west. Once again, we see Aries ruled by Mars, nd Libra ruled by Venus. To complete the square, we now see the gn of Scorpio opposite the sign of Taurus in the direction of east to est and opposite Libra from north to south. Scorpio is ruled by lars and Libra and Taurus is ruled by Venus.

The final diagonals which ascend from the bottom of each rner on the Cube of Space relay and circulate the intelligences of he Life Force of Chockmah through the planet Mars, as well as the reative image-making power of the planet Venus. **All of the final iagonals participate in this process.**

This current ascends from the domain of the High Priestess, fusing the Prima Materia with the Life Force and containing it in a essel of a specific creative image. The fact that all final diagonals ass through the center tells us that what ascends from the subcon- ious mind is rellay directed by the activity of the Central Ego, hich is at the center of the Cube.

The sign of Scorpio is the night throne of Mars. Scorpio rules eath and rebirth, as well as the sexual functions of the body. Both ries and Scorpio are ruled by Mars. Although they are not opposite the zodiacal year, they are located on diametrically opposite lines n the Cube of Space.

THE SIGN OF SCORPIO

Aries begins the zodiacal year with Mars ruling its first de-canate. The sign of Scorpio repeats this order.

As we saw the Chaldean order coming to a perfect end in Li-bra, the order ending with Jupiter, we see it begin with Mars in the sign of Scorpio. As with Aries, the sign of Scorpio has three plane-tary rulers:

Ph-Nun = Mars in Scorpio = 130
Resh-Nun = Sun in Scorpio = 250
Daleth-Nun = Venus in Scorpio = 54

MARS IN SCORPIO

The 5 of Cups represents the union of the intelligences of Mars in Scorpio. This particular Minor Key expresses the power of Mars like no other Key in the Tarot series.

By its number 5, the 5 of Cups is seated in the sphere of Geburah, sphere of Mars. This is the aspect of Mars as it works in the Briatic world, world of creative ideas. Whenever creative ideas are generated, the force of Mars is present.

The fact that the planet Mars is the ruler of this decanate, declares the presence of the intelligence of Mars.

Not only is Mars the ruler of the first decanate of Scorpio, it is also the ruler of the sign of Scorpio. This gives the 5 of Cups tremendous martian influence.

One other factor not often considered in this Key, is the co-rulership of Scorpio with the planet Pluto, the higher octave of Mars. It is also the Mother Letter which generates the Mars force from the center of the Cube.

The combined influences of Key 13, Death/Scorpio/Nun, Key 16, the Tower/Mars/Peh, and Key 20, Judgement/Pluto/Sheen, is the spelling of the word Nefesh, the Animal Soul. Furthermore, if we were to reduce the numbers attributed to these three letters,

Sheen = 300/3

Nun = 50/5

Peh = 80/8,

and place them in ratio form, 3:5:8, we would find the divine proportion which, which states the relationship between Nature, Humanity and God. This proportion is portrayed on the pentagram, symbol of humanity, and the star which the Wise Men followed to find the World Savior, or Messiah (MShICh), whose value is = 358 (the numbers of the divine proportion, and the reduced values of Seen, Nun, and Peh).

Through the powers of the pentagram, so prominently present in the 5 of Cups, we may understand the true nature of the **Serpent** of temptation, as the **Exalted light** of the **Anointed One**, **Renews** the mind **Of Humanity.**

NChSh - Nachash - Serpent

AVR MOLH - Aor Maalah - The exalted light

MShICh - Messiah - The anointed one

MChVDSh - Mekhodesh - Renewing

ANVShA -Anasha - Of men

These words have a value of 358, the value of the divine proportion of Pluto, Scorpio, and Mars, 3:5:8.

THE SUN IN SCORPIO

The 6 of Cups is the Minor Key which represents the union of intelligences of the Sun and the sign of Scorpio. There is a similar relationship between the 5 and 6 of Cups. Both these planetary intelligences are located within their own particular sphere. As the sphere of Geburah is the sphere of Mars, so the sphere of Tiphareth is the sphere of the Sun.

Key 13, Death, the Tarot Key attributed to the sign of Scorpio, shows the dissolution of forms outworn, as does the symbolism in Key 16, The Tower. These make up the 5 of Cups.

As there is the destruction and putrefaction of old forms, there is also the rising of the Sun in the background of Key 13. This is symbolic of what takes place when one completes the Great Work.

Before the Great Work is completed, there must be the breaking down of the form that is no longer useful. This brings in the alchemical operation of putrefaction.

A seed cannot send forth the **Great Light** unless the husks of the seed putrefy. As promised **Through Abraham, The Living God of Ages** would **Dwell** within the **Perpetual Laboratory** of humanity, and come forth as the Savior.

AVR GDVL - Aur Gawdol - A great light

BABRHM - Be-Abraham - Through Abraham

AL ChI HOVLMIM -El Chai Ha-Olahmim - Living God of Ages

MDVR - Mawdor - Dwelling

Laboratorium Perpetuum - Perpetual laboratory (Latin)

These words have a value of 250, the combined values of Resh/Nun, the Sun in Scorpio.

VENUS IN SCORPIO

As with the 5 and 6 of Cups, the 7 of Cups, Venus in Scorpio, is located in the sphere of its planetary influence. The sphere of Netzach is the sphere of Venus where the desire of the One is stepped down through the Central Ego into a vibration acceptable to the centers of expression in the world of Assiah. The desires we receive are the desire of the Central Self centered in all creation.

When a particular form is outworn, there is the need to replace it with a form that is suitable for the continuation of the Great Work. When one form is destroyed and there is no form to replace it, the environment for a rather tragic situation exists. A form worse that the one destroyed may be the replacement. Historically, we have seen this in national governments after a revolution has taken place. Citizens are often worse off than they were before the revolution.

The combined influence of Venus in Scorpio, the 7 of Cups, reveals the desire for the new form through creative images through the sphere of desire, Netzach.

Although the sign of Scorpio is ruled by the planet Mars, its intelligence speaks to the nature of Venus. The intelligence of Nun, the letter attributed to Scorpio, is the Imaginative Intelligence. Venus and the sphere Netzach are the agents of the Desire Nature. Another connection between Venus and Scorpio is the combination of the letters of Venus and Scorpio, Daleth/Nun. They spell Dan, the name of the 8th tribe of Israel, attributed to the sign of Scorpio.

From the mind stuff emerges a creative image, like a **Wall or Wave**, to bring forth from the **Quiet** formless deep a **Coagulated** form to declare the **Magnificence**, of the **Power of God.**

ND - Nahd - A Hill, Wall, forming on the water.[2]

DN -Dan - The Eighth Tribe of Israel

DMI -Demiy - Quiet

Coagula - Coagulate - To solidify

VGDVLH - Ve Gedulah - And magnificence

KCh IHVH - Kakh-Jehovah - The Power of God

These words have a value of 54, the combined value of Daleth/Nun, Venus in Scorpio.

The Sign of Sagittarius

The sign of the archer, Sagittarius, brings the zodiacal year into its darkest hour. On an alchemical level, it speaks to the operation of **Incineration.** The stages preceding Incineration appear to be performed by the alchemist himself through the agency of self-consciousness. Incineration is only accomplished through the **State of Grace,** and the presence of the Holy Guardian Angel, pictured in Key 14, Temperence.

On the Cube of Space, the letter Samek/Sagittarius is located in the west above line. This connects the intelligences of the Magian, Key 1, Mercury, self-consciousness, and The Wheel of Fortune, the planet Jupiter.

Jupiter rules the sign of Sagittarius and, hence, the operation of Incineration. Since the letter Samek is the Intelligence of the Test and Trial of Probation, there is a sense of being tested, as gold is purged of it dross through incineration.

Perhaps the greatest example of Jupiter ruling the sign of Sagittarius is through Final Kaph. Final Kaph ascends at the terminating points of Pisces, and Cancer at the southeast below corner. There the exaltation of Jupiter through the sign of Cancer mixes with the ruling quality of Jupiter from the sign of Pisces. Together they lend their influence through the center to the northwest above corner where the sign of Sagittarius begins, and circulates the subconcious qualities of Jupiter on the above face of the conscious mind. Here the great benefactor of Jupiter brings out the qualities of Higher Learning associated with the 9th house ruled by Sagittarius and the planet Jupiter.

The three decanates of Sagittarius are ruled by the planets:

Beth-Samek = Mercury in Sagittarius = 62

Gimel-Samek = Moon in Sagittarius = 63

Tav-Samek = Saturn in Sagittarius = 460

MERCURY IN SAGITTARIUS

The 8 of Wands is the Minor Key that represents the influenc
of Mercury in Sagittarius. The number 8 identifies this Minor Key
with the sphere of Hod on the Tree of Life. This is the sphere of Intellect, as it expresses itself in the Atziluthic world.

The combinations of Samek and Beth bring the aspirant into
another level of the alchemical process. As mentioned in the com-
mentary on Key 14, Temperence, Sagittarius, we find the operation o:
Incineration at work. This brings the aspirant into a greater awareness of the truth that "Unless the Lord build the House, they labor
in vain that build it."

The *Secret Doctrine* mentions that centers of expression gain a
sense of personal "I" due to the focusing of a **Ray** from the fiery Lif
Breath within a particular vessel.[3] As the vessel evolves, it is able to
hold and multiply the ray within itself. When this occurs, the Great
Work is completed.

Before this can happen, there must be a total purgation of all
dross left by the process of putrefaction, symbolic of Key 13, Death.
This is what sets up the environment for the awareness of the aspirant that, unless he enters into the state of Grace or **Conversation**

With the Holy Guardian Angel, there will be a sense of being stuck
at a certain point of the evolutionary process.

What takes place is the longing for aid, with the attitude symbolic of the two mendicants in Key 5, The Hierophant. The letter
Beth, The House, is supported and completed by what is represented by the Holy Archangel Michael, pictured in Key 14.

Through the power of the Great Angelic Alchemist, our personality is Tested, and the remaining dross is separated. This gives
us the Ability to Hold the ray of the Life Breath and Behold the Vision of The Lord.

BChN - Bahkan - To try, to test

HAVN - Hown - Ability, vigor.

VKVL - Vakool - Hold

BHNH - Bhinnay - Behold

BMChZH - Bamakhazeh - In the vision of the Lord

These words have a value of 60, the value of Mercury in Sagittarius,
and Beth/Samek.

THE MOON IN SAGITTARIUS

  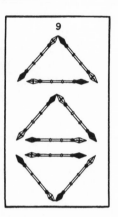

The 9 of Wands brings forth the intelligences of the Moon in Sagittarius through the letters of Gimel and Samek. This is the influence of the 9th sphere of Yesod, the sphere of the astral patterns in the world of Atziluth.

There is a similar relationship between what takes place in the union of Samek and Gimel, and what happens to the continental plates as they collide beneath the ocean's surface. The predominant plate, or the one that is slightly higher than the other, causes the below plate to be driven into the anterosphere, where it is melted by the heat of the earth's core, and is re-distributed upon the surface of the earth through volcanic activity. There, it creates new land forms, such as islands, or new layers upon the already existing land mass.

So it is with the subconscious mind stuff as it enters the alchemical operation of Incineration. It is the predominant suggestion originating at the above, or self-conscious level that determines which of the forms shall manifest. So the intelligence of Moon in Sagittarius incinerates the old patterns to allow the new form to come into manifestation for the refinement of the personality.

Through the state of **Grace, the Glory of God** shines forth through **the first Matter,** and **Establishes** the permanent Temple.

> HChN - Khane - The grace
>
> KBVD-AL - Kabode-AL - The glory of God
>
> VBNH -VaBawnaw - and establishes
>
> Magnesia - The First Matter

SATURN IN SAGITTARIUS

  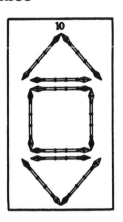

As the personality becomes transformed, self-consciousness
akes on another sense of beingness. By the aid of the Holy
Guardian Angel, our subconscious mind stuff is transmuted into
iner expressions of Divine Will. It is through the limiting power of
he 10 of Wands that these more refined forms come into being. Sat-
rn in Sagittarius is where the Lead (Saturn) is transmuted into the
old of Tiphareth.

The 9 and 10 of Wands shows us the Middle Pillar of the Tree
f Life. The intelligence of Gimel, shows us the Uniting Intelligence
vhich connects the Crown of Primal Will, Kether, to the sphere of
iphareth. The intelligence of Samek connects the sphere of
iphareth to the sphere of Yesod, sphere of the animal soul and Yet-
iratic patterns. The 10 of Wands, Saturn in Sagittarius, connects the
phere of Yesod to the world of manifestation through the path of
av, Saturn. This completes the particular phase of the Atzulithic de-
cent into the Malkuth of creative ideas, where the suit of Cups con-
inues the condensation of Spirit.

THE SIGN OF CAPRICORN

Key 15, The Devil, and the letter Ayin is perhaps the most mysterious of all the Major Keys and it represents the greatest of paradoxes. On the one hand, it shows the conditions of bondage to the outer sensorium. Fear and erroneous interpretations of the conditions of the world abound in the symbolism of this Key. Yet in spite of its outward appearance, Key 15 represents the first stage of Spiritual Unfoldment.[4] When conditions get bad enough in our lives, when we have experienced enough pain, something inside us moves away from the normal sense perception towards the desire of seeing beyond the surface of appearance.

The letter Ayin is also connected with the Prima Materia. In Genesis, Ayin represents the cardinal Earth, which is "To-Hu va Bohu", **Formless and Void.** The letter Ayin is connected with the Ayin of the Ayin Soph Aur, of which naught can be said. On one level, Ayin represents the immersion into matter, on another level, it is the infinite chaos which contains all potential in a unmanifested state. In the beginning God separated from **The Nothing** the heavens and the earth.

On the Cube of Space, Key 15, the Devil, is on the west below line. It receives the influence of Key 11, Justice, and Key 9, the Hermit. The line of Ayin is the place where the formation of our mind stuff through the power of suggestion greets us face to face. The conditions resulting from our images are played out on this west below line.

The planetary intelligences ruling the three decanates of Capricorn are:

Kaph - Ayin - Jupiter in Capricorn = 90

Peh - Ayin - Mars in Capricorn =150

Resh - Ayin - Sun in Capricorn =270

JUPITER IN CAPRICORN

The 2 of Pentacles is the Minor Key that represents the combination of Jupiter in Capricorn. On the Cube of Space, Jupiter in Capricorn holds a special relationship with the sign of Libra, for it occupies the same point as the 4 of Swords (Jupiter in Libra). On the northwest below corner, the intelligence of Libra flows into the sign of Capricorn bringing the exalted state of Saturn (Saturn in Libra) into the sign of rulership (Saturn in Capricorn). This occurs in the doubly- occupied point of Jupiter in Libra/Capricorn, (see Chapter 4, Figure 5).

The 2 of Pentacles represents the projection of the Life Force of Chockmah into the world of Assiah. In the sign of Capricorn, this manifests as the extension of **Light** (LVX) into the world of form. The expansive quality of Jupiter fills the vessels, in which the Life Force is projected. The vessels are ruled by the limiting power of Saturn. In this Key, the memory of the infinite potential of the Life Force is brought to bear upon the physical plane.

Through the agency of Jupiter in Capricorn, the great **King** of Chockmah brings forth the creative **Waters** from the **Foundation** of existence, to create vessels for **Our Redeemer,** who is the **Heart of the Stone.**

MLK - Melek - King

H-ISVDH - Ha Yesod - The foundation

MIM - Mem - Water

GALNV - Goalenu - Our redeemer

LB-HABN - Laib ha-Ehben - The heart of the stone

These words have a value of 90, the combined value of Kaph/Ayin, Jupiter in Capricorn.

MARS IN CAPRICORN

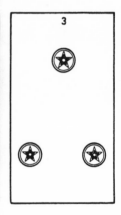

Mars in Capricorn is represented by the 3 of Pentacles. This presents a most interesting as well as difficult combination of astrological influences. Since Mars and Saturn are traditionally difficult bedfellows, we find a hard paradox to reconcile. In spite of the difficulties attributed to this combination,[5] we find that Saturn rules the sign of Capricorn and Mars is the **Exalted** planet. The fact that **The Devil** is the Tarot Key attributed to the sign of Capricorn, is a good indication of the difficulty between the Saturn/Mars union. When one is able to reconcile the difficulty, then a great lesson is learned concerning the Great Work. The 3 of Pentacles is seated in the sphere of Binah (sphere of Saturn). Once again, we must remember that Saturn is the secret abode of fire, and Mars is the planetary manifestation of the release of this fire.

During the time period of Capricorn, we have no trouble experiencing the saturnian qualities of the winter. It is the Mars qualities that are less obvious. In spite of the appearance of things, Mars

busy at work preparing the seeds and soil for what must take
lace when the winter months turn into spring.

By the power of **The Most High God,** the **Hidden Stone** is re-
ealed by the **Scraping Away** of the **Clay** which conceals the great
;ift **of God,** the **Savior of the World.**

ALHA OLIA - Eloha Elyah - Most High God

Occultum Lapidem - Hidden stone

BSChPh - Sakhap - To scrape away

BChSPh - Khashaf - In clay

Nathanel - Gift of God (Greek)

Salvator Mundi - Savior of the world.

hese words have a value of 150, the combined value of Peh/Ayin,
Iars in Capricorn.

THE SUN IN CAPRICORN

  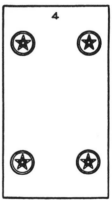

The combination of the Sun in Capricorn is represented by
ie 4 of Pentacles. The 4 of Pentacles is seated in the sphere of
hesed, where the personal as well as collective memory is stored.
he merging of these two intelligences shows us the entire spectrum
f the formation of humanity, the birth of the world Savior and the
ucifixion of the Savior upon the cross.

First of all, when the Sun enters the sign of Capricorn, it cre-
:es a line of demarcation from the continual growth of darkness, as
en in the sign of Sagittarius, to the emergence of the light at the

Winter Solstice. Metaphorically, the light of the Son/Sun or world saviors are born in the sign of Capricorn.

Second, it is through the Magic Square of Saturn that the 36 decanates, now under consideration, receive their placement on the Cube. If we refer back to Figure 9 of Chapter 2, we can see the numbers 1-9 on each face of the Cube of Space. Each face adds up to the number 45, the number of Adam.

On Figure 8 of Chapter 1, we see the unfolded Cube formed into a a cross, symbol of Saturn, and the crucifixion of the Savior. When all 6 faces of the Cube are multiplied, 6 x 45 = 270, we have the value of the letters I.N.R.I., which was the sentence of death issued to Jesus as he was nailed onto the cross.

Through the **Limiting** power of Saturn, the **Light of the Sun** descended into form so as to shed the **Blood of the Lamb**, upon the cross, for the Salvation of Humanity.

> STRA - Sitra - Limit of the sun
>
> ALPH-LMD-PhH - Aleph, spelled in full
>
> HAVR HChMH - Aur ha-Khammaw - Light of the sun
>
> VDM-KR - Dam-Car - Blood of the lamb
>
> ADM - Adam - 6x45=270

These words have a value of 270, the combined value of Resh/Ayin, the Sun in Capricorn.

THE SIGN OF AQUARIUS

Continuing with the march of the zodiacal year, we come to the sign of Aquarius. This sign is represented by Tarot Key 17, The Star. Its location on the Cube of Space is the south above line, which brings into activity the aspects of the above face, self-consciousness, Key 1 The Magician, and the southern face, Key 19 The Sun. The alchemical function of Aquarius is dissolution. This is taking the particular material of the work and placing it into solution. Furthermore, the activity of meditation is the key function of Tarot Key 17, The Star, and the letter Tzaddi. Both Dissolution meditation are represented by the two wavy lines we have come to understand as representative of the astrological symbol for Aquarius.

There has been an interesting journey of the intelligence of Saturn as it descends the currents of Libra and then is picked up by the currents of Capricorn and delivered to the southwest line of Aquarius by the ascending currents of Scorpio. Not only does the sign of Scorpio bring the intelligence of Saturn into the sign of Aquarius, but it also brings the exalted qualities of Uranus into its sign of rulership. We see the birth of Aquarius in the symbolism of the seed in the upper right hand corner of Key 13, Death; in the human figure in the upper right-hand corner of Key 21 Saturn; and the focus of the gaze of the Fool towards the upper right hand corner in Key 0.

Here, at the southwest corner, the combined forces of Uranus and Saturn, the Alpha and Omega, the Aleph (Uranus) and Tav (Saturn), come together in the sign which is the promise of the New Age.

Through the power of meditation, the exalted qualities of Uranus are lifted into equal partnership with the form-giver Saturn.

The fish hook of Tzaddi (Key 17, The Star) is cast into the fixed waters of Scorpio, and the fish (Nun) is pulled into consciousness, where the will of the One is revealed to humanity.

> The passage from the death and darkness of the
> Outer
> Into the life and light
> Of the Inner
> Is but the turning of the eye of the soul
> From the contemplation of appearance
> To the vision of reality.[6]

VENUS IN AQUARIUS

The 5 of Swords represents the combined influences of Venus in Aquarius and the letters Daleth and Tzaddi. The 5 of Swords is located in Geburah of Yetzirah, seat of Divine Will in the world of action. In the western mysteries, we are taught that the Divine Will is expressed through the **Will to Create** new forms of expression. This takes place through the agency of Humanity (Aquarius) and through the powers of creative imagination (Venus), in the sphere of Geburah. This Will to Create is revealed through the alchemical process of dissolution and meditation.

The illusion of personal effort is ultimately dispelled through continued meditational practice. We come to know that we are not the meditator; we are being meditated upon. In this realization, we become like the **chickpea** in Rumi's poem, **A Chickpea to Cook.**

A Chickpea to Cook

A Chickpea leaps almost over the rim of the pot
where it's being boiled.
Why are you doing this to me?
The cook knocks him down with the ladle
Don't you try to jump out.
You think I'm torturing you.
I'm giving you flavor,
So you can mix with spices and rice
and be the lovely vitality of a human being.
Remember when you drank rain in the garden.
That was for this."
Grace first. Sexual pleasure,
then a boiling new life begins,
and the Friend has something good to eat.
Eventually the chickpea
will say to the cook
"Boil me some more
Hit me with the skimming spoon.
I can't do this by myself.
I'm Like an elephant that dreams of gardens
back in Hindustan and doesn't pay attention
To his driver. You're my cook, my Driver,
my Way into Existence. I love your cooking."
The Cook says,
I was once like you,
fresh from the ground. Then I boiled in time,
and boiled in the Body, two fierce boilings.
My animal-soul grew powerful.
I controlled it with practices
and boiled some more, and boiled
once beyond that.
and became your Teacher."[7]

And so it goes with us. The great alchemist boils us, seasons us, and dissolves us, until we become ready for this great feast to become a lovely vitality for **Divine Nourishment.**

Through the attention and guidance of **The Driver of Unities,** our **Spirits become free from Guile,** hence, becoming **Perpetual Bread** for the nourishment of the Divine Will. We consciously **Perceive the Truth** from the **Inner Voice,** that we are One with **The**

Stone of the Wise, and the **Mediating Influence.**

> HMNHIG HAChDVTv - Ha-Menahig Ha-Achadoth - The driver of unities.

> AIN BRVChV RMIH - Ayin Beruacho Remiyah - In his spirit no guile.

> HLChM TvMID - Lekhem Tawmid - Perpetual bread

> He-noetike aletheia - The truth perceived (Greek)

> BTv QVL - Bath Kol - Inner voice

> H-ABN HChKMVTv - Ha-Ehben ha Chokmoth - The Stone of the wise

> BShPhO NBDL - BeShepa Neobedal - Mediating Influence

These words have a value of 538, the extended values of   Daleth and Tzaddi,

$$Daleth=[D(4)+L(30)+Th(400)] = 434$$
$$TzDI=[Tz(90)+D(4)+I(+(10)] = +\underline{104}$$
$$538$$

MERCURY IN AQUARIUS

  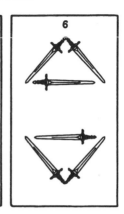

Mercury, ruling the second decanate of Aquarius, is repre-
ented by the 6 of Swords and the sphere of Tiphareth in the world
f Yetzirah.Since Aquarius is an air sign, Mercury is well-placed.

There is a special relationship between Mercury and Aquar-
us as ruler of the second decanate.

There are nine instances in the astrological wheel where a giv-
n planet rules a particular decanate in both the Chaldean and tradi-
ional placements of the planets, (See Chapter 3 Page 10). These are :

Mars in Aries

Sun in Aries

Saturn in Taurus

Jupiter in Leo

Mars in Leo

Saturn in Libra

Mars in Scorpio

Mercury in Aquarius

Mars in Pisces

In these nine instances, there are only two occasions where
he ruler of a given decanate rules the first and last dwadashama of
hat decanate. These are Jupiter in Leo and Mercury in Aquarius.
upiter in Leo rules the second decanate as does Mercury in Aquar-
us. These two decanates occur at opposite times in the year and ac-
ivate the Aquarius/Leo axis on the great zodiacal wheel. On the

Cube of Space, Jupiter in Leo is north above, Mercury in Aquarius is south above. The dwadashamas in the second decanate begin with the sign of Sagittarius and end with the sign of Pisces. Both of these signs are ruled by the planet Jupiter.

The second decanate of Aquarius begins with the sign of Gemini and ends with the sign of Virgo. Both of these signs are ruled by Mercury, and the sign of Virgo is also the sign of exaltation of Mercury.

As a matter of interest, these two times of the year occur during the cross-quarters of Lammas and Candlemas.

Besides these interesting correlations and relationships, Mercury in Aquarius shows the use of self-consciousness in the operation of meditation, symbolized by Key 17 The Star, the Tarot Key attributed to Aquarius. It is the power of self-consciousness which chooses the subject of meditation and keeps the focus of the mind on the subject at hand.

Within the **Clay** vessel of humanity, we are meditated upon. There **The Everlasting Father,** fills the vessels with **The All Glorious Creative Powers.**

BTz - Botz - Whitish clay

HABI-AD -Ha-Abi-ad - The everlasting Father

VELHIM - VaElohim - The creative powers

These words have a value of 23, the value of Beth+Tzaddi.

THE MOON IN AQUARIUS

  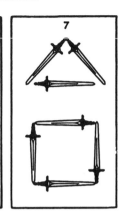

The 7 of Swords is the Minor Key representative of the Moon in Aquarius. This is the sphere of Netzach in the world of Yetzirah.

As the planet Mercury in Aquarius creates the focus for the process of active meditation, so the Moon represents the reservoir of personal and collective memory. This memory is accessible through an act of intention originating at the conscious level and applied in the operation of meditation.

The Moon in Aquarius also represents the scene depicted in Key 17 The Star, where Isis is **unveiled**. The inscription on the temple of Isis states, "I, Isis, am all that has been, that is or shall be, no mortal man hath ever me unveiled."[8] Through the operation of mediation, Isis does indeed unveil herself willingly to those who will learn the laws of nature.

Mythologically, Isis was the sister/bride of Osirus. She brought him back to life and projected his spirit into the form of Horus, the Sun/Son. In Key 2, The High Priestess, which holds the attribution to the Moon, we see a figure crowned with the crown of Isis.

We read in the Emerald Tablet, **"The Moon is its Mother."** Through the Uniting Intelligence of the High Priestess, we learn that **All is from One.** From this One, we receive **Our Inheritance** of Love.

Luna Mater - The Moon is its mother (Latin)

Omnia ab uno - All is from One (Latin)

NChLH - Nakhelah - Inheritance

Agapeh - Spiritual love (Greek)

These words have a value of 93, the combined value of Gimel and Tzaddi, The Moon in Aquarius.

THE SIGN OF PISCES

The sign of Pisces holds many of the mysteries of the Great Work. It is the end of the zodiacal year and brings the cycle of travel on the Cube of Space to closure, until the next journey is taken on.

In Key 18 The Moon, we see the Path of Return leading beyond the limitations of natural man into a new way of being.

The letter Qoph is assigned to the sign of Pisces and it governs the function of sleep. Alchemically, the letter Qoph is associated with the operation of multiplication. Multiplication is likened to a fire, which when well-tended, may be used to ignite countless more flames.

Jupiter and Neptune are the co-rulers of the sign of Pisces and Venus is the planet exalted. We find the entire cycle of the east-west axis at work in the planetary intelligences of Pisces.

Neptune and the letter Mem is the axis which extends from the center to the east and from the center to the west. The boundary of the eastern face of the Cube generates the intelligence of Venus. The creative images of Venus come forth from the east and manifest in the west, where the intelligence of Jupiter is waiting in the letter of Kaph, the hand in the act of grasping.

As mentioned in an earlier chapter, the south below line of Pisces brings the experience of what took place in our encounter with Key 15 The Devil, on the west below line and joins it with the incredible complexities of the southeast below corner where the influences of Cancer, Taurus, and Pisces come together. At this point there is no control, no choice, of where to take our experiences into consciousness.

SATURN IN PISCES

Saturn in Pisces is represented by the 8 of Cups. This is the sphere of Hod in the Briatic world, world of creative ideas.

There are some interesting connections with the sphere of Hod, Neptune and Saturn. Since the sphere of Hod is on the pillar of Severity, it receives influence from the sphere of Saturn which is at the head of this pillar. The 23rd path of Mem (Neptune) is the path which energizes the sphere of Hod, as the intelligence of Binah descends through the Paths of Cheth, Geburah, and Mem. Furthermore the 26th path of the Renewing Intelligence, Key 15 The Devil, is the path which connects the sphere of Tiphareth to the sphere of Hod. This is another connection to the intelligence of Saturn , for Saturn rules the sign of Capricorn, the 26th path.

On the Cube of Space, the sphere of Hod is attributed to the southern face of the Cube.[9] It is on the southwestern below line where the current of Pisces resides. It is on this line that the influence of Hod, Key 19 The Sun, and Key 2 The High Priestess, merge. The sign of Pisces is where the **"Sun and Moon" become alchemically joined.** Through the intelligences of Saturn and Pisces, the **First Matter,** becomes the **Foundation** for the **Holy of Holies, the Abode of Peace.**

PhVK - Pook - First matter

IVD SMK VV DLTh - Yesod - Foundation. (Yesod spelled in full)

IRVShLM - Jerusalem - Abode of peace

JUPITER IN PISCES

Jupiter in Pisces is represented by the 9 of Cups. This is the Lord of Abundance and Compassion operating in its sign of rulership. In the sphere of Yesod and the 9 of Cups, the true relationship between Jupiter and the Moon come into view. Both Jupiter and the Moon work together in the control of bodily functions under the directorship of automatic consciousness. The sphere of Yesod is the seat of the animal soul, which is the director of automatic consciousness. We see this harmonious working relationship hinted at in the Briataic[10] color attributions given to the sphere of the Moon and sphere of Jupiter on the Tree of Life. In the sphere of Chesed, Jupiter receives the color blue associated with the Moon; and in the sphere Yesod, the Moon receives the color violet, which is attributed to Jupiter.

Pisces is the Corporeal Intelligence. This is where the glimpses of higher conscious, perceived in earlier stages of unfoldment, are incorporated into the cellular consciousness of the physical body, thus multiplying the consciousness of the "**New Order**."

Through conscious understanding of the intelligence of Jupiter in Pisces, a center of expression becomes **The Chosen One**, who was **Refused by the Builders**, thus uniting **Christ, God and Man** in the form of a **Stone**. The old patterns are **Broken to Pieces**, making way for **The New Order of the Ages.**

> BChIR - Bawkhiyr - One chosen
>
> MASV HBVNIM - Mahasu ha-Bonim - Refused by the builders
>
> Christus, Deus et Homo - Christ God and Man (Latin)

Lapis - Stone (Latin)

NPhTz -Nahphatz -To break to pieces

Novus Ordo Seclorum - New Order of the Ages

These words have a value of 220, the combined values of Qoph and Kaph, spelled in full (KPh + QPh).

MARS IN PISCES

Mars in Pisces is represented by the 10 of Cups. This combination brings the zodiacal year to a close, where it is picked up by the sign of Aries initiating a new year at the Spring Equinox. This is the time of year where an extra boost of martian force is needed to bring the inertia of the winter into the activity of the spring.

The 10 of Cups is Malkuth in the Briatic world. It is the clear image in the Divine Mind of the plan for humanity. On the Cube of Space, it is the southwest below point. This point is doubly ruled by Mars, for it is also the ascending southwest corner of Scorpio. Here both the 4 and 10 of Cups have jurisdiction. The 4 of Cups takes the influence of Capricorn to the above face, and the 10 of Cups continues the current around to complete the navigation of the below face.

If we bring our attention to the three paths on the Tree of Life, descending into the sphere of Malkuth, we can see the combination of the sign of Pisces in the 29th path, Saturn in the 32nd path, and Pluto in the 31st path.

We have already discussed the 8 of Cups, Saturn in Pisces. The planet Pluto is of the Mother letter Sheen, which is the letter that generates the planet Mars. We find these letters Sheen and Qoph bringing together the intellectual and desire nature into the sphere of Guph, Malkuth.

On the Cube of Space, we see this take place on the southwest below corner where Pluto, the letter Sheen, ascends through the sign of Scorpio, its sign of rulership; and Pisces, traversing the south below line and rejoining Pluto in Aquarius as the influence of Pisces rises through the sign of Taurus.

The combination of Mars in Pisces, makes way for **The Light of the Sun,** as it comes forth from the **Primordial Sea,** which shines upon the earth and prepares it for spring.

AVR H-ChMH - Aur ha Khammaw - Light of the sun

IM HQDMVNI - Primordial sea (Name for the sphere of Saturn)

These words have a value of 265, the combined values of the extensions of Qoph and Peh (QPH + PhH).

This completes this section on the combination of Letters making up the decanates of the zodiacal year.

FOOTNOTES

[1] The spirit of Saturn is exalted in the sign of Libra and is ruler in the sign of Capricorn, Key 15, The Devil.

[2] The explanation of this word speaks of a formation of something solid upon the waters. **Gesenius**

[3] Writings of Dr. case, *TF: 31* p4.

[4] Dr. Paul Foster Case. *TF: 33-34*

[5] Liz Green, *Saturn, a New Look at a New Devil*

[6] *The Book of Tokens,* by Dr. Paul Foster Case. Meditation of Tzaddi.

[7] *Delicious Laughter,* Poetry of Rumi, versions by Coleman Barks.

[8] *Secret Teachings of All Ages* by Manly Palmer Hall

[9] *OT-10:3* by Dr. Paul Foster Case.

[10] There are four color scales. Each of these scales represent one of the worlds of Qabalah. The Briatic color scale is the scale most often encountered. This is the scale used by the B.O.T.A., and Golden Dawn, in their color attributions of sound and color to the Tarot Keys, and the Tree of Life.

CONCLUSION

WHAT NEXT?

he past 7 chapters have presented a great deal of material concerning the Cube of Space. These chapters have defined the parts of the Macrocosmic Cube as well as the 27 microcosmic cubic units. The combination of the Macrocosmic and Microcosmic cubes define a cosmology using the Chaldean Aleph-Beth and the pictorial vehicle of the 22 Major Trumps and the 56 Minor Trumps of the Tarot. Working with these symbols sets up the environment for the transmutation of the psycho/physiological dross of our "personal vehicles." Transformation should be the number one goal of all aspirants in the Great Work. There really is nothing else so important as the refinement of our vehicles.

This work has outlined and named the parts of the Cube of Space so that a more clear image of the process of manifestation and transmutation can be visualized. Placing these symbols on the Cube of Space or the Tree of Life assists us in focusing upon the specific area we wish to target. The main idea is to limit ourselves in our work so as to methodically transmute that which is not yet fine.

The model of the Cube of Space can be expanded to encompass the entire universe, condensed to deal with our world system, or be condensed even further to deal with our own physical bodies or perhaps even to work on an atomic level.

Although this work has brought some new ideas to light concerning the Cube of Space, there is much more work to be done. Each student that reads this work will be affected in different ways. Some will say, "So What!," while others may be inspired to look deeper not only into the form itself, but into ways in which the form, can be used practically.

Because of the infinite scope of this work, no book will ever exhaust all there is to know about the Cube of Space. It is therefore prudent to invoke the limiting power of Saturn and bring this phase of this work to closure.

This is an invitation to all who have been drawn into the western mysteries, to take this work and add to it. The following ideas are areas under consideration by the author and are presently "up for grabs."

SATURN

The individual relationship between Saturn and all other planets warrants close attention. One of the reasons for this can be seen in the system of **Tattwas.**

In the Vedic symbol system of Tattwas, Saturn is given the attribution of AKASHA.[1] From Akasha all things come and to Akasha all things return. Akasha is associated with the principle of hearing, and it is also associated with pure Space. This is analogous to the Sphere of Binah which sets aside the space or container into which manifestation takes place.

The idea of Saturn being the matrix from which all forms are derived and to which all forms return brings up a very interesting relationship between the seven sacred planets and the Cube of Space, which is defined by the Magic Square of Saturn.

Since the 12 lines of the Cube are defined by the 12 simple letters which represent the 12 signs of the zodiac, it becomes evident that the Cube would be inscribed in the heavens as the 12 signs are traversed by each planet.

There are other cubes formed when one addresses the various cycles of conjunction between planets. The conjunctions that seems most important are those connected to Saturn. The one conjunction that seems most interesting is the Saturn/Neptune conjunction. There is a great deal of work being done in relationship to this conjunction at present.

In chapters 6 and 7 we dealt with the combinations of letters residing on the points that make up the Magic Square of Saturn. These letter combinations are an outward manifestation of something that has begun within the center of the Cube of Space. This something can be traced to the workings of Neptune and Saturn. Neptune and Saturn are two different expressions of one mode of Intelligence: the Intelligence of the **One,** as it is expressed both in form, (Saturn), and in the formless, (Neptune). This Intelligence is whole and perfect, and creates centers for its self expression.

Within the center of the Cube, rest the letters Tav and Mem, associated with Saturn and Neptune respectively. Together they spell **Toom** in Hebrew, meaning perfection, wholeness, completion.

The two spirals held by the cosmic dancer in Key 21, Saturn, present the separation and return of consciousness. Consciousness separated from the formless and void and enters into the world of time and form. After developing experience, it then returns to its source. We see a similar spiral in the rope suspending the Hanged Man, Key 12, associated with Neptune.

In Chapter Two we have read *The Emerald Tablet of Hermes,* which is a statement about the law of correspondence. **That which is above is as that which is below, and that which is below is as that which is above.** We have also learned that, that which is within is as that which is without. With this knowledge we can gain an understanding about the things that go on within our being, and the relationship to the things that go on outside our being. We can relate things that occur on the most subtle of levels to the things which take place on astronomical levels. Once you know how to swim it doesn't matter whether the water is four feet or one thousand feet deep. The principles by which we enter into an understanding of the cosmic order, are the same no matter at what level we are focusing our attention.

Since the six directions of the Cube: north, south, east, west, above and below, create boundaries for the impact of Divine forces, we can go to these boundaries and witness the impact of Saturn/Neptune as they march in majesty along the currents of the interior of the Cube of Space.

THE CYCLE

It takes approximately 30 years for the planet Saturn to travel through the twelve signs of the zodiac. Most everyone reading this book will be well acquainted with what is called the **Saturn Return**. This occurs when the planet Saturn returns to the natal location at the time of an individuals birth. This usually takes place when we reach the age of 30, and our whole world tends to be shaken from one end to the other. It is Saturn, the form giver saying "So what about all the lies you have been accepting as the truth? It is time to get UP and get to work!" It is the Soul playing reveille.

Neptune, on the other hand, takes about 164 years to traverse the heavens. There are few individuals who have actually seen the complete Neptune cycle. We can, however, experience different aspects of it.

When Saturn and Neptune join forces on the exterior of the Cube of Space it is called a Saturn/Neptune conjunction. This conjunction takes place every 36 years. The theory is that when the two planets are aligned, there is a re-evaluation of the conditions on the exterior of the Cube in relationship to the perfect pattern which has been projected from the center. How is the plan that originated at the center been doing in the world of manifestation? What distortion has taken place? How does the manifested product differ from the perfect Divine act of intention?

We can take a historical look at these conditions and gain a sense of the impact of the forces projected by Saturn/Neptune, or we can look at the concept of the Fall from the Garden, and see how the form that was created in the image and likeness of God is faring as a living conscious creator.

There are other planetary relationships which need to be considered. Saturn distributes its influence on the other six sacred planets, and therefore is the chief **Administrator** in our world system. This administration connects with the Intelligence attributed to the letter Tav, the **Administrative Intelligence.**

In predictive astrology, it is the distribution of Saturn over the other six planets which gives us clues as to what type of challenges lie ahead. All of these challenges are administered by the powers of Saturn, into the container of the Cube of Space.

We will not go any further into this idea at present. It is mentioned to give the reader food for thought.

Another area of consideration is working with the Angelic vibratory formulas that are assigned to the 36 decanates located on the boundaries of the Cube of Space.

Since the Cube of Space is a vessel which receives the influences of the other nine sephiroth, it is associated with the earth. If one was to orient the Cube with the earth, we would find places on the earth that would correlate with the points of the Cube and hence with the Angelic forces assigned to those points.Once again there will be no further development of this idea in this container.

It is the hope of this author that this work will bring some inspiration to those who wish to go further into the uncharted waters of occult work. There are many areas of study that have been started by so many of the practical occultists of the 19th and 20th centuries. These areas need to be examined and further developed. It is time for the students of the past generations of teachers, to come forth

and make their contributions. These contributions will carry the
Torch of Wisdom into the 21st century, and bring us ever closer to
the fulfillment of the Aquarian Age.

FOOTNOTES

S and C, Lesson 8, page 1 pp. 3, by Paul Foster Case.

 IBLIOGRAPHY

had, Frater, *The Anatomy of the Body of God*, New York: Weiser, 1969.

had, Frater, *Q.B.L. The Bride's Reception*, New York: Samuel Weiser, 1969.

had, Frater, *The Egyptian Revival*, New York: Samuel Weiser, 1973.

bertus, Frater, *The Alchemist's Handbook*, York Beach, Maine: Samuel Weiser, 1981.

onymous, *Meditations on the Tarot*, New York: Amity House, 1985.

onymous, *Praxis Spagyrica Pholosophica*, Salt Lake City: Paracelsus Research Society, 1966.

ily, Alice, *Esoteric Astrology*, New York: Lucis Publishing Co., 1951.

ily, Alice, *Discipleship in The New Age*, New York: Lucis Publishing Co. 1954.

ily, Alice, *A Treatise on Cosmic Fire*, New York: Lucis Publishing Co., 1951.

avatksy, H.P., *The Secret Doctrine*, Pasadena, California: Theosophical University Press, 1977.

amen, Jacob, *The Three Principles of Divine Essence*, Chicago, Ill, Yogi Publication Society, 1909.

se, Paul Foster, *The Book of Tokens*, Los Angeles, Ca.: Builders of the Adytum, 1934.

se, Paul Foster, *The Tarot*, Richmond, Va.: Macoy Publishing Co. 1947.

se, Paul Foster, *The True and Invisible Rosicrucian Order*, New York, New York: Samuel Weiser, 1985.

rlot, J.E., *A Dictionary of Symbols*. New York: Philosophical Library, 1974.

rowley, Aleister, *777*, York Beach, Maine: Samuel Weiser, 1973.

rowley, Aleister, *The Book of Thoth*, York Beach, Maine: Samuel Weiser, 1969.

Fortune, Dion, *The Mystical Qabalah*, London: The Society of Inner Light, 1957.

Godwin, David, *Godwins Cabalistic Encyclopedia*, York Beach, Maine: Samuel Weiser. 1979

Gray, William, *The Ladder of Lights* York Beach, Maine: Samuel Weiser, 1968.

Gray, William, *Western Inner Workings* York Beach, Maine: Samuel Weiser, 1983.

Green, Liz, *Saturn*, York Beach, Maine: Samuel Weiser, 1976.

Hall, Manly Palmer, *Masonic Orders of Fraternity*, Los Angeles, Ca.: Philosophical Research Society, Inc., 1950.

Hall, Manley Palmer, *The Secret Teachings Of All Ages*, Los Angeles, Ca.: The Philosophical Research Society, Inc., 1972

Hillman, James, *Archetypal Psychology*, Dallas: Spring Publications, 1983.

Hoeller, Stephan, A. *The Royal Road*, Wheaton, Ill.: The Theosophical Publishing House, 1975.

Junius, Manfred M., *Practical Handbook of Plant Alchemy*, New York: Inner Traditions, 1979.

Jung, Carl, *Archetypes and The Collective Unconscious*, Princeton: Princeton University Press, 1968.

Kaplan, Aryeh, *Meditation and The Bible*, New York: Samuel Weiser, 1978.

Kaplan, Aryeh, *Meditation and The Kabbalah*, New York: Samuel Weiser, 1982.

Kaplan, Stuart,R. *The Tarot, Vol. 1 and 2*, New York: U.S. Games Inc. 1978-1988.

Knight, Gareth, *The Practical Guide to Qabalistic Symbolism* York Beach, Maine: Samuel Weiser, 1983.

Lawlor, Robert, *Sacred Geometry* New York: Crossroad, 1982.

Leadbeater, C.W., *The Hidden Life In Freemasonry*, India: The Theosophical Publishing House, 1926.

Levi, Eliphas, *The Book of Splendors*, New York: Samuel Weiser, 1973.

Levi, Eliphas, *The Great Secret*, Wellingborough, Northamptonshire: The Aquarian Press, 1975.

evi, Eliphas, *The History of Magic*, New York, New York: Samuel Weiser, 1969.

evi, Eliphas, *Transcendental Magic*, London: Rider, 1984.

lackey, Albert G., *Encyclopaedia of Freemasonry*, New York: The Masonic History Company, 1925.

lagnus, Alabertus, *The Book of Secrets*, London: Oxford University Press, 1973.

lathews, John and Caitlin, *The Western Way*, vol 1, and 2, London: 1986.

he *Nag Hammadi Library*, New York: Harper and Row, 1977.

'ichols, Sallie, *Jung and The Tarot*, York Beach, Maine: Samuel Weiser, 1980.

oken, Alan, *Soul-Centered Astrology*, New York: Bantam, 1990.

agels, Elaine, *The Gnostic Gospels*, New York: Random House, 1979.

once, Charles, *Kabalah*, London: Quest Books, 1973.

agoczy, Comte De St. Germain, *La Tres Sainte Trinopophie*, Los Angeles, Ca: Philosophical Research Society, 1983.

egardie, Israel, *The Golden Dawn*, St. Paul, Minnesota: 1982.

egardie, Israel, *The Tree of Life*, New York: Samuel Weiser, 1971.

obbins, Michael D. *Tapestry of The Gods*, Vol. 1 and 2, Jersey City Heights, New Jersey: The University of the Seven Rays Publishing House, 1990.

udolph, Kurt, *Gnosis*, San Francisco: Harper and Roe, 1977.

udhyar, Dane, *The Astrological Houses*, Garden City, New York: Doubleday, 1972.

araydarian, Torkom, *Symphony of the Zodiac*, Sedona, Arizona: Aquarian Educational Group, 1988.

uares, Carlos, *The Cipher of Genesis*, Boulder: Shambhala, 1978.

hree Initiates, *The Kybalion*, Chicago, Ill.: Yogi Publishing Co., 1940

cholem, Gershom, *Kabalah*, New York: New American Library, 1974.

he *Sepher Yetzirah*, Translated by Kaplan, Aryeh, York Beach, Maine: Samuel Weiser, 1990.

he *Sepher Yetzirah*, Translated by, Suares, Carlos, Boulder, Colorado.: Shambala, 1976.

The Sepher Yetzirah, Translated by Westcott, W. Wynn, New York: Samuel Weiser, 1980.

Waite, Arthur Edward, *The Brotherhood of the Rosy Cross*, New York: University Press.

Waite, Arthur Edward, *The Hermetic Museum*, New York: Samuel Weiser, 1973.

Waite, Arthur Edward, *A New Encyclopedia of Freemasonry, Vol. 1, and 2.* New York: Weathervane Books, 1960.

Waite, Athur Edward, *The Illustrated Key to the Tarot*, Chicago, Ill.: de Laurence Company, 1918.

Waite, Arthur Edward, *The Turba Philosophorum*, New York: Samuel Weiser, 1973.

Wang, Robert, *The Qabalistic Tarot*, York Beach, Maine: Samuel Weiser, 1983.

The Zohar, New York: Rebecca Bennet Publications.

INDEX